Ditch. Dare. Do!

P9-DEI-726

Ditch. Dare. Do!

3D Personal Branding for Executive Success

66 Ways to Become Influential, Indispensable, and Incredibly Happy at Work!

William Arruda

Deb Dib

Copyright ©2013 by William Arruda and Deb Dib. All Rights Reserved.

Published by TradesMark Press International
New York, NY, USA

This publication or any part thereof may not be copied, reproduced, stored in a physical or electronic retrieval system, or transmitted in any form by any means, electronic, mechanical, photocopying, scanning, recording, or otherwise, except as permitted under Section 107 or 108 of the 1976 United States Copyright Act, without either: (1) the prior written permission of the publisher, or (2) authorization through payment of the appropriate per-copy fee to the Copyright Clearance Center, 222 Rosewood Drive, Danvers, Massachusetts, 01923, (978) 750-8400, fax (978) 646-8600, or www.copyright.com.

Limit of Liability/Disclaimer of Warranty:

While both authors and publisher have used their best efforts in preparing and producing the book, they make no representations or warranties with respect to the accuracy or completeness of the contents of this book and specifically disclaim any implied warranties of merchantability or fitness for a particular purpose. No warranty may be created or extended by marketing or sales representatives or in print or online sales and marketing materials. The advice and strategies contained herein are the opinions of the authors and may not be suitable for your situation. You should consult with the proper professional where appropriate. Neither the publisher nor the authors shall be held liable for any loss of profit or any other commercial damages, including but not limited to special, incidental, consequential, or any other damage.

Library of Congress Cataloguing-in-Publication Data:

Arruda, William, 1961 – Ditch, dare, do: 66 ways to become influential, indispensable, and incredibly happy at work / William Arruda, Deb Dib

Includes index.

ISBN 9781620504574

First Edition.

Book cover by: Stacey Aaronson
Book design by: Ryan Torres

Acknowledgments

I tell everyone I'm the most fortunate person I know because there are so many loving, fascinating, and inspirational people in my life—family, friends, colleagues, and clients who help me be a better version of myself. The list is too long—you know who you are! Thanks, too, to the careerists whom I meet at companies all over the world who want their work to have meaning and dare to be their authentic selves. And I'd like to express my gratitude to the Reach-certified Personal Branding Strategists (hundreds of committed coaches and consultants) and my dedicated Reach team. They have put their faith in Reach and in me. I truly appreciate it. Lastly, I want to thank all the contributors to this book for their meaningful stories, quotes, and insights and the witty and wise Deb Dib, without whom this book would not exist. Her brilliance, flexibility, and focus made this writing project fun, fulfilling, and fruitful.

—William Arruda

My life, my career, and my joy are powerfully tied to family, friends, colleagues in the careers and personal branding communities, and my wonderful clients—you're far too numerous to mention by name, but you know who you are! I am so thankful for your presence in my life, your courage to be real, and your inability to accept the status quo! You feed my soul, creativity, and energy—and affirm my belief that purpose, passion, and innovation (and, yes, profit), even in baby steps, can ultimately move mountains and change the world. I must especially thank my family—Doug, Patrick, and Jessamyn—and my dear friends: Chandlee Bryan and Susan Whitcomb (of The Academies); Kim Batson, Cindy Kraft, Beverly Harvey, and Jan Melnik (my C-SuiteCareerCatalysts.com colleagues); and Pat Schuler (my fabulous coach). Without your support and understanding, I could never have "played hooky" to finish this book. And of course, there's William, my teacher, mentor, and friend—your personal brand training and belief in me changed my life forever.

—Deb Dib

FOREWORD

The business world, these days, is divided into those who like the concept of branding and those who don't. (Among the latter is Jonathan Salem Baskin, with his sardonic book, *Branding Only Works on Cattle*.) Personal branding, as a concept, was born unnoticed in 1937 in a book by Napoleon Hill and reborn in 1997 by Tom Peters, while experts on branding, such as Dan Schawbel and William Arruda, appeared thereafter.

Now, those who like the concept of personal branding will rush to get their hands (or eyes) on this book, since one of the authors is William Arruda—yes, that William Arruda. Anything from his pen (or keyboard) is bound to be valuable from the get-go. And his coauthor, Deb Dib, is equally famous in the branding world.

So, let me speak to the other people, the ones who don't like the phrase "personal branding," and, seeing that this is a book on "branding," might at first sight decide not to buy or read it.

My basic concern is that you dig deeper and understand that personal branding is not merely some modern fad but an ancient concern, only dressed here in modern language. It is the concern of the snowflake and of your fingerprints. The theme is "uniqueness." No two complex snowflakes have ever been found to be identical, nor have any two people's fingerprints. From the creation of the Earth and of humankind, uniqueness has been the driver.

"Personal branding" is simply a matter of answering these questions: What makes you unique? How do you express your uniqueness? How do you gain a reputation so people will understand that your uniqueness makes you valuable to them?

Be clear about this: That uniqueness resides in the person, not in the product. The thing we produce, each of us, whether it be ideas, or services, or things, is only the outward expression of that internal uniqueness which resides in each of us. So, don't be put off by the vocabulary. "Brand" is just another word for "what is unique about you."

"The tools of branding" is just another phrase for "the playgrounds where we exhibit and act out our uniqueness." The playgrounds are new, since 1996, and that is the value of this book: It enumerates them and discusses how to use them—Facebook, LinkedIn, Google+, Twitter, images, video, YouTube, blogs, thought leaders' blogs, professional associations, etc.—in brief, two-page chapters, for fast reading and slow digestion.

What we end up with here is a book for both "branding people" and "non-branding people." I hope you will read it and find it valuable. I hope you discover or rediscover your uniqueness. For that is what makes you so valuable as a human being.

In that process, I hope you become infinitely more aware of what makes others unique. For that is what makes you valuable in whatever community or communities you may happen to find yourself, from this time forth.

Dick Bolles, author
What Color Is Your Parachute? 2013
A Practical Manual for Job-Hunters and Career-Changers
10 million copies sold; rewritten annually

CONTENTS

INTRODUCTION

Control Your Destiny!

KNOW. SHOW. GROW!

Your fast track to becoming an influential, indispensable, and incredibly happy executive starts here.

Why? Because 3D personal branding unlocks your *full* potential, *freeing* you to give your best and be your best. Your 3D personal brand *is* YOU—a clarified, confident, and compelling you—you with a *unique* promise of value. Your personal brand is your trusted reputation; it's what people can expect from you, always. It's at the intersection of what's authentic to you, what differentiates you from your peers, and what influences those who are making decisions about you.

3D personal branding allows you to reap happiness, fulfillment, and success—to live in fabulous 3D—in your work, in your life, and in your world. And a workforce of authentically branded employees is good for your company, too—it helps your company grow stronger, more authentic, and more trusted. Building your brand can help you achieve all of that and more—if you have the courage to ditch, dare, and do!

3D personal branding is purposeful and magnetic. It's never spin, but it is strategic. It helps the people who need you to find you. And in a world where decision-making is increasingly complex and swift, your personal brand is your career compass, guiding you to your true north, simplifying decision-making into one profound question: Is this on-brand for me?

Is 3D personal branding for you?

Do you want to be comfortably, confidently, and authentically YOU—always and everywhere?

Are you burning to do something different but don't know what it is? Or do you just want more of the great work and life you already have? Has success at the top of the pyramid eluded you or come too slowly? Or are you there but finding that the top is not what you expected?

Do you want to make your teams great and your company greater? Are you famous within your organization but faceless outside of it? Are you a hero to your team but feel like you're just not on the radar of the people who can help you attain your goals? Are you the iconic square peg in a round hole, but your boss doesn't know it and keeps promoting you into wrong-fit positions?

Are you struggling with work-life balance? Are you a mom or dad trying to be the best you can be at work while doing the best you can at home? Or are you a stay-at-home parent or caregiver recalibrating your life while building your skills and visibility for re-entry?

Are you working around the clock, sacrificing precious personal or family time to protect your position in an uncertain economy, yet still feeling like you're tottering on the edge of the precipice? Or are you unexpectedly unemployed or underemployed—unsure of your direction and far outside of your executive comfort zone?

Do you want to make a difference? Do you want to do something special in the world? Do you want to leave an enduring legacy? Do you want to do these things but can't find the time or the vehicle? Or do you simply want to be fulfilled at work and happier in your life?

We find that most executives relate to one or more of these questions, and sometimes their challenges are even more daunting. No matter your situation, we can tell you from coaching and training thousands of personal branding executive clients (including many in the Fortune 100) that the personal branding strategies in *Ditch. Dare. Do!* work.

3D personal branding is the key—for you *and* your company!

Branding boldly and practically, 3D-style, gives you permission to be yourself—your best self—to know that YOU are like no other (and to have your company know that, too!).

In the words of Dr. Seuss, *"Today you are You, that is truer than true. There is no one alive who is Youer than You."* You should trust that YOU are enough—that your particular combination of strengths, passions, and talents is exactly what is needed, and you build upon that—for yourself, your organization, and your teams. That's why *Ditch. Dare. Do!* is subtitled *66 Ways to Become Influential, Indispensable, and Incredibly Happy at Work*. Branded executives are fully and powerfully themselves, set firmly on a trajectory to ever more success and happiness at work (and in life and the world, too!).

Before, the company brand was everything. Remember the "company man" of the not-too-distant past? Today, the individuals working in the company are the authentic face of the brand, not the reverse. Employees' brands and their company's brand are inextricably linked. The workforce itself is a part of the company's marketplace strategy.

The most successful companies recognize that employees are human brand assets. You need only view recent ad campaigns like GE's "Pass the Wrench," IBM's "I'm an IBMer," and Intel's "Star" (featuring Ajay Bhatt) to see that these companies get it. All of these ads showcase employees as the brands' greatest resources—the true value of the company.

These companies know that when employees understand and apply their individual brands to the corporate mission, they create differentiation in the marketplace, build their constituencies' trust, impact the bottom line, and win the game.

In a white paper from the Economist Intelligence Unit and the IBM Institute for Business Value, Chris LeBlanc, corporate marketing manager at 3M Australia, asserts, *"[We've entered] an era of collaboration and information-sharing and transparency, in which every employee has become a touch point. Everyone is responsible for communicating the company's values, products and services. We are all messengers."*

Your personal brand is that important!

How to Use This Book

The Ditch. Dare. Do! Guide

We wrote *Ditch. Dare. Do!* with executives like you in mind.

You know you can never stand still; you know you need to know more and be more to achieve and surpass your goals. You know you need to manage your career *inside* your organization as well as in your world—to build an internal brand that positions you for best-fit upward momentum that serves you and your organization. You know you need to be branded (or at least you've heard you should be), but your overloaded schedule makes "busy" seem like a vacation! You're too busy working *in* your career to work *on* your career or your brand.

We know your world—its triumphs and its troubles—because through the personal branding process, we're granted entry into the worlds of our executive clients. We get to know them on a profound and trusted level—we know what they do, what they face, and what they want, and we're privileged to witness how personal branding catalyzes their careers and their dreams.

You'll meet a number of our personal branding stars throughout this book—some by real name, others by pseudonym—and we hope their experiences will help you see that you, too, can "be a brand!" And we'll share some of our own experiences in using personal branding to stand out. You'll see that we practice what we preach.

We purposely designed *Ditch. Dare. Do!* to be a bold and *brief* real-world instruction manual for continuously managing your career and achieving unstoppable momentum. Does it provide deeply specific, step-by-step instructions for all the nuances of branding? Nope. We wanted to give you a book you'd actually read, not one you'd avoid until you could fit it into your schedule.

Ditch. Dare. Do! is deliberately succinct, designed to be read in one sitting or in brief bursts. But don't let our brevity fool you—you'll learn exactly what you need to do to know, show, and grow your brand. In fact, we're so dedicated to maximizing your time while you're building your brand that we even tell you how to start doing it in just nine minutes a day! (More on that later.)

Our only caveat? No matter how eager you are to "dip in and do," read the chapters in the order in which they are presented. Each chapter builds on the information and actions presented in previous chapters. It's hard to be patient, but don't let urgency inhibit understanding.

We designed *Ditch. Dare. Do!* to be conversational, quick, and primed for action—to nurture new ideas and stimulate execution.

Ditch. Dare. Do! is organized into three main sections—KNOW, SHOW, GROW—and a brief "take action" section, GO. Each covers a seminal aspect of the personal branding process.

Part One, KNOW, is all about *you*. You'll learn to become introspective. You'll begin to understand what makes you, YOU, by looking inward and by seeking feedback about your professional reputation. But take courage in hand, because authenticity doesn't come easily. Be patient, because before you get to the good stuff, like building loyal fans or getting that big promotion, you need to take the time and do the work to be clear about who you are and where you want to go. And bring your wellies: Discovering and refining your brand gets muddy before it gets clear.

Once you're clear, it's on to **Part Two, SHOW**. In SHOW, it's not about you anymore! Here, the focus shifts to *others*—the people who need to know you so you can reach your goals. You'll identify them and develop leading-edge, branded communication materials you can use to inspire, engage, intrigue, influence, attract, and _____ (put YOUR preferred verb here!).

Part Three, GROW, is about you *and* them. You'll start to toot your own horn—without bragging—to go from invisible to ever-present. You'll learn how to build your personal promotion plan and execute it in support of your goals. You'll be real, you'll be virtual, and you'll be known online and offline. You'll go from "Who?" to "Must know!" to "WOW!"

Finally, to help keep you focused and turn learning into action, there's **Part Four, GO.** GO outlines the most critical actions you must take to move your brand and career forward on the fast track or whatever the right track is for you.

Here's how it works:

Each KNOW, SHOW, and GROW section starts with a QUICK QUIZ to assess the strength of your brand and then explores key concepts in six to eight action-inspiring chapters.

Every chapter of every section contains three SNAPS—two-page, stand-alone executive brand topics designed to fit your schedule, spark your interest, and prime you for action—and they can be read in a "snap."

Each SNAP ends with a DITCH, a DARE, or a DO challenge:

- A *ditch* replaces thinking and habits that aren't helping you move forward.
- A *dare* propels you to take new, exciting risks.
- A *do* is a critical step you must execute to build your brand.

Each chapter of three snaps is followed by a page designed to capture your SPARKS. Sparks are "ditch, dare, and do" ideas that come to you as you read—ideas that will spark action.

When you reach the end of each KNOW, SHOW, GROW, and GO section, you'll find a Go-time Grid where you can capture, refine, and prioritize your sparks to create an action plan.

Here's the best part: as you read, you'll be building your personal brand plan. And when you're finished, you'll have four Go-time Grids ready to roll it out. That's *Ditch. Dare. Do!* action!

To your 3D success!

Follow the *Ditch. Dare. Do!* 3D brand plan to *your* executive success—in the book and on the companion website: www.ditchdaredo.com. In a few minutes between meetings, on the subway, in the airport lounge, or in a few spare moments on the weekend, dip into *Ditch. Dare. Do!,* read a few snaps, and create a few sparks. Or settle into your easy chair or your beach blanket and read it through.

It's up to you. Read it fast; read it slow. Spend nine minutes a day or nine hours a month. Then make your action plan and invest some time in the most important priority on your calendar: YOUR brand.

Regardless of your approach, you'll be equipped to out-compete, out-perform, and manage your career in the new world of work. You'll be able to contribute to your organization while expanding your career success. You'll be more contented personally and more fulfilled professionally. You'll be influential, indispensable, and incredibly happy at work!

Sound good?

The Ditch. Dare. Do! Nine-Minute Brand Plan

If, despite our best efforts to make *Ditch. Dare. Do!* fit your busy life, you're starting to feel a bit overwhelmed, take a breath; you're not alone. The idea that significant "branding time" is required each day prevents many executives from doing *anything* to manage their career. It's just another thing piled high on a mountain of commitments. But we have a solution!

William has developed a revolutionary concept: Just nine strategic minutes each day doing small but meaningful actions is all you need to manage your brand and advance your career. He recently presented his "Nine-Minute Brand Plan" in a white paper produced for LinkedIn, and overworked, double-booked, never-a-spare-moment professionals (and the media) took notice.

Here's why: We all desperately want to manage our careers, but the endeavor feels too complex and time-consuming to break into small actions. So we don't do anything, and we feel frustrated and guilty about it. We keep putting it off until we have time. And usually we don't have time until we lose a job or a promotion. *Then* our career becomes the priority that captures our time and attention.

Yet, consider this: little things add up. Committing to nine minutes every workday amounts to nearly 40 hours a year of steadfast focus on moving your brand forward. That's the equivalent of taking off a full week of work (or using a whole week of vacation) to invest time in career development—something most of us will never do. But each of us *can* invest nine minutes a day.

As you use the Go-time Grid action plan worksheets to record the ditches, dares, do's, and sparks most valuable to you, assign them a priority, and identify a date by which you plan to complete them. Then break them into smaller tasks that can be completed in nine minutes and schedule (at least) one every day.

If you're tempted to skip days, remember, doing this for a year is like spending an entire week focused on the single most important thing that will advance your career and happiness—the brand called YOU. Make it a habit, like brushing your teeth or working out—a non-negotiable commitment to your brand's health.

For additional ideas on using your nine minutes, you can join the conversation at the Nine Minutes a Day LinkedIn group.

Can you spare nine minutes a day to be influential, indispensable, and incredibly happy at work?

How Strong Is Your Brand?

The Ditch. Dare. Do! Brand Calculator

Before you dive into *Ditch. Dare. Do!*, take this quick quiz to see where your brand stands now. Are you a potential brand, rising brand, super brand, or even a mega brand?

You can take the abbreviated quiz here or the complete version of the quiz at www.ditchdaredo.com/quiz

1. Can you state your top five brand attributes—the most relevant and compelling adjectives that describe you?

   ☐ Yes ☐ No

2. Have you identified and documented your short- and long-term career goals?

   ☐ Yes ☐ No

3. Do you know what those around you would identify as your greatest strength?

   ☐ Yes ☐ No

4. Do you have a "So what? Make me care!" brand positioning statement that describes what you offer, and for whom, how you are different, and what value/ROI (return on investment) your differentiation creates?

   ☐ Yes ☐ No

5. Can you clearly describe your target audience—those people who need to know about you so that you can achieve your goals?

   ☐ Yes ☐ No

6. Do you have a home on the web that showcases your success, such as your own website, personal portal (i.e., about.me or flavors.me), etc.?

   ☐ Yes ☐ No

7. Do you infuse every project meeting, report, etc. with your personal brand—with what you want to be known for?

   ☐ Yes ☐ No

8. Have you proactively done something valuable for a member of your network this week?

   ☐ Yes ☐ No

9. Do you have a trusted focus group of peers, managers, or clients to provide honest personal brand feedback?

   ☐ Yes ☐ No

10. Do you have an area of thought leadership or specific point of view for which you are known?

    ☐ Yes ☐ No

Scoring

Count the total number of times you answered "Yes" to the questions and use the table below to see the current status of your brand.

"Yes" Responses	You are a:
0–3	**Potential Brand**—Your brand has potential, but you're not reaching it. (But you bought this book, so we know you understand the importance of personal branding.) Read *Ditch. Dare. Do!* for a powerful jump-start!
4–6	**Rising Brand**—You understand the importance of your personal brand and how it can help you expand your success, but you still have a way to go to achieve Mega Brand status. A strong brand will enable you to greatly expand your success, *Ditch. Dare. Do!* will help you keep the momentum growing!
7–9	**Super Brand**—Your brand is in great shape. You understand the concepts of branding and the importance of having a personal brand. You recognize that professional success requires that you stand out from your peers and be visible to those people who will help you expand your success. Now, it's time to take your Super Brand and turn it into a Mega Brand! *Ditch. Dare. Do!* action steps will propel you!
10	**Mega Brand**—Bravo! You're in great company. Take a moment to bask in your glory—then continue branding. Branding is not a one-time event—it requires continuous, deliberate effort. Keep reading *Ditch. Dare. Do!* for strategies that will keep your brand at the top!

GLOSSARY

To make *Ditch. Dare. Do!* relevant for you, today's learner, we redefined some common words to develop a new set of terms for the personal branding process. These terms act like a "cheat sheet," making it easy to remember the critical elements you need to build your brand and career.

Dare

(n) A challenge to take, a risk to up your game

(v) To boldly embrace a challenge

Ditch

(n) A habit or mindset that is no longer working or relevant

(v) To eradicate an archaic habit or mindset

Do

(n) An action you need to take to build your brand and advance your career

(v) To deliberately perform a brand-building activity

Go

(v) To act; the *Ditch. Dare. Do!* call to action

Go-time Grid

(n) A brand-focused do-list that houses your brand-building activities, priorities, and due dates

Grow

(v) To take action to expand your brand, your network, and your success

Know

(v) To uncover who you are, what makes you exceptional, and what makes you relevant and compelling to the people who are making decisions about you

Show

(v) To let the world see who you are—to be the authentic YOU

Snap

(n) A brief, action-compelling vignette

Spark

(n) A trigger that reminds you of brand-building actions you will take

KNOW

What Makes You, YOU?

Quick Quiz

Be a Brand

Be Real

Be Incomparable

Be Grounded

Be Relevant

Be Courageous

Be Deliberate

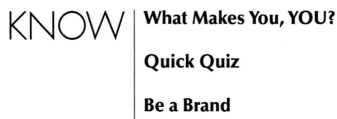

Be Whole

Know Your Brand:

What Makes You, YOU?

The most successful executives invest time in introspection—they are both self-assured *and* self-aware. Yet most of us don't spend much time being introspective. We focus on answering our emails, responding to voicemails, and participating in a seemingly endless number of meetings and conference calls.

You can't use who you are to get what you want if you don't *know* who you are or what's important to you. What are your top five values? What's your vision? What's your purpose?

In our work with executive clients, we find that most are not truly self-aware—even those who are wildly successful. They haven't had time for introspection; it's not a priority for them. They often come to us for coaching on creating or improving their brand communications, increasing their visibility, and enhancing their executive presence, and are surprised to find the internally reflective part of the personal branding process to be the most valuable. It forces them to take a step back and really get to know themselves, often for the first time. They've come for the "punch line" but find they love the "setup."

Be introspective. Understand what truly motivates you. Take time to understand who you are, what drives you, and what ROI value you create when you do what you do. Doing so is an essential step in the executive branding process.

Are YOU self-aware? Use the 24 snaps in Part One, KNOW, to discover and know the brand called YOU.

QUICK QUIZ

Before you jump into KNOW, rate how well you know yourself.

Rate your self-knowledge!				
Strongly Disagree				**Strongly Agree**
I know and apply my strengths regularly.				
1	2	3	4	5
I am clear about my reputation (what others think about me).				
1	2	3	4	5
I have a clear mission and goals for my career.				
1	2	3	4	5
I am in great physical shape.				
1	2	3	4	5
I am passionate about what I do.				
1	2	3	4	5
I know my values and live them every day.				
1	2	3	4	5
I know how to contribute to the company brand every day.				
1	2	3	4	5

Total: ______

Now, add up your score. Did you score a 35? Even if you did, we promise you, reading and taking action on the concepts in this section—KNOW—will help you get clarity about the brand called YOU. But if, as most executives do, you scored less than 35, *Ditch. Dare. Do!* is for you!

Chapter One | Be a Brand

KNOW

Promote Yourself!

Build Your Company

Attract Opportunity

Be Your Own Boss:
Promote Yourself!

You control your destiny.

Reality check: In the new world of work, building your brand is *not* optional. You are one of numerous executives with similar credentials competing for the same positions. No matter what the hierarchical structure is in your profession or organization, you are your own boss. No one else is there to take care of you. No one else will pull you to the top—not your manager, not the CEO.

In this competitive and rapidly changing executive environment, the only constant—the only security—is your brand and the value it promises and delivers. Power and momentum come from you and only from you!

Not long ago, your employer took control of your career.

As long as you conformed and didn't make too many waves, you could stay with a company for thirty years and retire with a pension. Now, on average, executives change positions every three years, companies every four years, and industries every five years. Yet, surveys tell us that most executives spend less than 5% of their time doing any form of career management. It's no wonder many executives feel adrift: they're navigating without a map.

But not all executives relinquish career control while they're busy working. They don't wait for their company to notice their strengths; they seize the wheel and steer their career. These executives develop a career blueprint that's good for them and good for their company.

Deb worked with an executive whose goal was to move from his position in a multinational company headquartered in Europe to a senior role leading an innovation center in China and then to a position in the C-suite. He didn't wait for it to happen—he put a plan in play. He requested global assignments, led the global sales team, developed innovation summits in China, fostered a culture of exploration within his teams, and earned an advanced degree at a leading international business school. He now leads the innovation center in China and is in line for a C-level role. The company is fully engaged with this top performer, and he is living his dream.

Proactively managing your brand is good for you and good for your company. When you take control of the choices you make about the positions you take, the way in which you handle challenges, the degree of effort you apply to your position, the way you present your intellectual and emotional assets, and the people you position as your allies and manage as your opponents, you shape and ensure your professional success. It is entirely up to you.

Are you ready to take control of your career? To place your career in good hands? YOUR good hands?

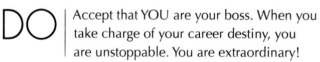

DO | Accept that YOU are your boss. When you take charge of your career destiny, you are unstoppable. You are extraordinary!

Build Your Brand: Build Your Company

If you're not managing your brand, you're not doing your job.

Your company needs you to build your brand! As companies increasingly realize that business is truly a human endeavor, they acknowledge that each employee has an impact on the success of the organization's brand.

As an executive, your brand reinforces and enhances corporate brand attributes. A strong executive brand helps you make a mark on your organization, augment your company's image and reputation, and increase your visibility and presence with all stakeholders inside and outside the walls of your organization.

One of William's clients, a senior associate at a professional services firm in Chicago, learned that *he* is the brand—in his clients' eyes (and those are the eyes that count!)—when one of his clients said to him, "I don't hire a consulting company, I hire a consultant. You are that consultant. To me and the members of my team, *you* are the company."

Your organization knows this. Your organization wants you to understand what makes you exceptional, use your brand value to deliver on the corporate brand promise, and be a visible leader with a solid reputation, confidently representing your company 24 hours a day.

And don't think this applies only to external-facing employees like consultants or salespeople; whether you're in purchasing, accounting, or the IT department, you, too, have clients. Having a strong brand builds solid connections with these clients—and solid connections are good for business and just make work more fun. The bonus for you? The people who have the strongest brands in the company are the people who get noticed and rewarded.

Building your brand inside your company and in the marketplace has become even more critical with the rise of social media. Social media has changed everything. Its immediacy and ability to connect customers and companies has forced businesses to become more human and more responsive. Customers and clients expect connection. Companies' brands are now built on connection. Your brand enables connection, both inside and outside the organization.

Are you ready to accept that having a strong personal brand is good for your company?

DITCH

Ditch the "personal" vs. "corporate" brand mindset. Both brands are inextricably linked. The connection powerfully supports corporate and career goals. Double winners! Go team!

Promote the Corporate Brand: Attract Opportunity

You don't have to be the CMO or the VP of marketing to impact the corporate brand.

Brands build trust, trust builds loyalty, and loyalty yields competitive advantage. And isn't that what you and your company want? Your company's brand is important to its success, and companies value people who help them succeed.

When you walk into an Apple store, the employees you meet seem to have a much bigger role than their jobs. Whether they are "geniuses," sales associates, or one-on-one training experts, their knowledge of and passion for the brand goes far beyond the role they are assigned. You just know they have their finger on all things Apple. They *exude* knowledge and pride. They are Apple-bred brand ambassadors.

Early in his career, William worked in branding at Lotus in Cambridge, MA (his best corporate job ever, he says). Part of his job was to ensure brand consistency—and for Lotus, one of the most important and differentiating attributes was "irreverent." One day, an HR colleague stopped by his office and told him, "We're building a new website where employees can go to get information about their 401(k). We want everything we do for employees to reflect the brand, so let's brainstorm some irreverent ideas for the name of the website." After a few short minutes, she shouted, "dontblowyourretirement.com!" and the name for the website was born. You can't get more irreverent than that!

Like William's HR colleague, move outside the regular hierarchy and appoint yourself as a self-made brand ambassador—for your team, your colleagues, your business partners, your external stakeholders. Know your company's top five brand attributes, brand positioning statement, and brand differentiation. Then think about how you can bolster the brand. Partner with your marketing colleagues to infuse the corporate brand into everything you do in your organization.

In a Gallup survey, employees were asked to assess their agreement with this statement: "I know what my company stands for and what makes our brand different from our competitors'." Only 41% of employees strongly agreed.

Don't be one of the 59%! Distinguish yourself as a brand ambassador. Brand ambassadors elevate themselves to a new level. Their role extends into every sector of the company or organization. Being a steward for the brand gives you another opportunity to connect with others throughout the company; it enables you to increase your visibility, demonstrate your commitment, and attract opportunities.

Brand ambassadors inspire and stand out. YOU want to stand out, don't you?

DITCH | Stop thinking branding belongs exclusively to the marketing department. YOU are the marketing department. Decide how you can impact the corporate brand. Stand out!

My Sparks

Record your ideas, sparked from Chapter 1.

Chapter Two

Be Real

KNOW

Be YOU!

Be Goal Oriented

Be Passionate!

Be the Real Deal:
Be YOU!

All strong brands are founded in authenticity. Branding is *not* spin.

Done right, branding is genuine. Unique. Real. It's not packaging or creating a false image for the outside world. Being YOU is empowering, energizing, attractive, and satisfying. It is the driver that helps you deliver value to your employer. It is the key to successful branding.

Oscar Wilde once quipped, *"Be yourself; everyone else is already taken."* To truly be yourself you must know who you are, where you want to go, and what drives you. You must also understand others' perceptions of you. Only after deep introspection and regular pursuit of feedback can you gain true knowledge of yourself and true clarity about your reputation.

That clarity—that authentic comfort in your own skin—builds a confidence that is magnetic to others. We all know people at work who radiate authenticity and confidence, and we like to be around them. They are natural leaders; they make us feel better and do better.

Sometimes being yourself is as simple as taking your passions to work. If you leave what you love at the door, you're incomplete. People sense that you're inauthentic, not because you're playing a role, but because you're not fully you.

Deb worked with a client who was a calm, quiet leader. He felt his career had leveled off because he was not seen as an energetic driver. Yet in his off-time, he was an expert marathon runner, downhill skier, and motorcycle racer. And in every sport, he was an intense and deliberate planner. For example, when planning his marathons, he determined exactly how and when to train, and plotted every nuance of the course—when to sprint, when to rest, when to take water breaks. He completed every one of the 14 marathons in which he competed—and finished some in fewer than three hours! He and Deb made a plan to weave his marathon running into his leadership style. His personal mantra "Set the pace to win the race" became a professional persona that connected his marathon methodology to his business ROI. What some had misinterpreted as a plodding management style was soon appreciated by teams and leadership as a clearly valuable, trusted asset. Score!

Anne Morrow Lindberg said, "The most exhausting thing you can do is to be inauthentic." Use your authentic self—your values, passions, and vision—to guide your career and lead your team. You'll become a magnetic "must-have" resource.

Shakespeare wrote, "To thine own self be true." Are you ready to let people know who *you* really are?

DARE | Stop being who you think people want you to be. Just BE. Really. Try it. You are SO worth it!

Focus on the Future:

Be Goal Oriented

Executive brand management starts with focused aspiration.

As an experienced executive, you start every project with a goal. But have you established the goals for your career? And we aren't talking about the commitments your company asks you to write each year!

Just as a business plan guides your company, your career goals give your brand direction. Without goals, you lack the focus necessary to turn an unknown brand into a clear winner, and a solid job history into a stellar career.

We often speak with executives whose default goal is to be VP, become partner, or make it to the C-suite. But when they think long and hard about it, they find that's often *not* what they're really after.

What *do* you want? What do you *really* want?

The first step in executive brand management is to start at the beginning by visualizing the end. Once you know where you want to go, you can identify milestones that can get you there. And you can turn those milestones into actionable steps that you can take every day—moving you closer and closer to your ultimate goal.

William started his company, Reach, with the singular goal of putting personal branding on the map. With that goal in mind, he steadfastly focused on the milestone that would make it happen: Connect 10 million people, in 10 years, to the Reach personal branding methodology.

To enable his goal he planned key action items:

- A non-stop global public speaking schedule
- Building the Reach certification program (transforming coaches and HR executives into Reach personal branding experts)
- Raising the program's visibility (by joining several career and executive coaching networking groups, delivering keynotes at career conferences, writing *Personal Branding for Coaches*, and more)

William's focus on a clear milestone and specific actions made it easy to say no to opportunities (however enticing) that would detour him from his goals; for example, when he was offered several corporate branding consulting gigs, he immediately referred them to others in his network so he could continue to attract and train a community of personal branding professionals who would rapidly extend his voice and accelerate his goal. Today, there are hundreds of Reach-certified Personal Branding Strategists in 31 countries, and they have been instrumental in putting Reach Personal Branding on the map.

Like William, when you identify your goals; keep them fresh and visceral; and engage in daily, deliberate brand management, even the most audacious dreams can be achieved.

Do you know where *you're* going? Are your daily decisions direct routes to goals, or off-brand detours to distraction?

DITCH | Document your goals; they are your treasure map—the guide to your richly satisfying future. Post them where you'll see them, and read them every day. Your goals are gold!

Passion Is for the Bedroom *and* the Boardroom: Be Passionate!

Passion is fuel. Fill 'er up!

When you connect what you do, who you are, how you do what you do, and what you want, there is no end to where you can take your career!

You need only look at the most successful people in the world to see that this is true. Think Mark Cuban, the late Steve Jobs, Richard Branson, Oprah, Lady Gaga, Michael Jordan, Jimmy Fallon, and Bobby Flay. Whether a business tycoon, an innovator, an adventurer, a media mogul, an entertainer, a sports giant, a comedian, or a chef, each of these individuals is known for extreme, single-minded passion.

Combining your passions with your experience is the ideal way to direct your career and fully engage in your work. That's what Chris Shirley does every day as a global communications manager for one of the world's largest banks. After ten years of working on Wall Street, Chris quit his job and began an intensive filmmaking program at NYU (with nothing more than a completed screenplay to recommend him).

Chris quickly realized that writing, not directing, was his passion, and that his screenplay might actually work better as a novel. While his agent was flogging his novel, a friend asked him to help write a financial plan for his publishing company—spurring Chris to wonder if there was a way to combine his finance expertise and his love of writing. Five weeks later, after a referral from a friend, Chris was hired as a global communications manager and gets paid to write every day.

Even if your passion isn't exactly what you do every day, you can find creative ways to connect your passion to your career. If you're passionate about the environment and work in accounting, you might develop a program to save the company money by introducing environmentally aware practices. If you're passionate about healthy eating, you might work with your company cafeteria to come up with a healthy eating option every day, or initiate a health challenge program for members of your team—or even your company.

In a recent workshop, William asked participants to brainstorm ways they could bring their passions to work. Although initially skeptical about bringing his passion for cooking to his job as a finance executive, one participant had a breakthrough: He immediately scheduled his first Breakfast Brainstorm, after his workshop table partner suggested that he could combine his brand attribute of "collaborative" with his passion for cooking by preparing a breakfast or lunch for his team meetings. Another participant started a company choir and holds for-fee events, using the proceeds to benefit local animal shelters.

Your passion motivates, inspires, and guides you (and your teams) to extraordinary heights, propelling your career to the next level (even if your present career isn't your calling). Spend some time brainstorming ways to inject your passion into everything you do at work. Fervor and energy are contagious!

How can you ignite YOUR passion?

DITCH | Bring your passion to work. Passion makes leaders, and passionate leaders are inspiring leaders! Use YOUR passion to inspire!

My Sparks

Record your ideas, sparked from Chapter 2.

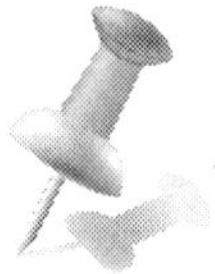

Chapter Three

KNOW

Be Incomparable

Be Extraordinary

Be Memorable

Be Loved

Don't Be Fine:

Be Extraordinary

When it comes to succeeding in today's competitive marketplace, the word "fine" is a four-letter word.

Fine, adequate, average, okay, acceptable. Do you want *your* work to be described with these words? If your reputation is fine, you're in trouble. People rarely get excited in life about things that are "fine," and they rarely have emotional connections to them. "Fine" doesn't position you to win the Executive of the Year award.

Replace the word "fine" with "great" and strive for greatness by leveraging your strengths, rather than improving on your weaknesses. If you have a weakness that will impede your success, work on it, but if it won't get in the way of your success, ignore it!

Maximize your strengths; become known by them and build your personal brand around those things that make you different and interesting. If you are the most creative CIO, focus on that. If you are the most ethical, efficient, and organized finance director, make that more visible. If you are the zany team leader who gets all of the company functions' attendees talking and laughing, be more of that.

When William was working in London, a copywriter on his team was a real jokester—with an incomparable, amazingly quick wit. William noticed that although the copywriter's humor was on display with his peers and enjoyed by all during team meetings, it was greatly subdued with internal clients and senior leaders. William encouraged him to share his witty quips in meetings with senior executives, and the copywriter soon became known for this attribute throughout the company.

Knowing your strengths not only builds your brand, but also helps you stay on course. Travis, a supply-chain executive, was deeply aware of his strengths (each tied to people and relationships) and how they impacted his performance and job satisfaction (aka happiness!). He was offered a promotion that required none of his strengths, and he convinced his manager *not* to promote him into the role, explaining that the company would be losing the greatest value he delivered. Shortly after his manager heard this rational business case, he found Travis a perfect-fit leadership position in another part of the organization. He's now cheerfully working in his sweet spot at least 90% of the time—a win-win for him and for the company.

As Sir Arthur Conan Doyle wrote, "Mediocrity knows nothing higher than itself, but talent instantly recognizes genius." Be outstanding, be audacious, push the envelope. Never settle for adequate. When you apply your strengths to everything you do, you raise yourself far above "fine." You become great, excellent, exceptional, extraordinary. And that's how you want to be known, isn't it?

What will position you to win the Executive of the Year award?

DARE | Deliberately ignore weaknesses that don't impede your success. Identify your TOP strengths. Build on them. Your strengths are the drivers that excite you and propel your career.

Focus on One Thing:
Be Memorable

All strong brands focus on something, not many things.

In branding, less is more. Focus steadfastly on the *single* strength you've chosen to drive your brand. You'll be in good company!

Walmart is known for low prices, Apple is all about innovation, Nordstrom equals exceptional service. It's the same for strong personal brands. Jack Welch led GE to tremendous success through his intuition. Bill Clinton used his outstanding communication skills to secure two terms in office, despite scandal. Richard Branson applied his intrepid style to building a multibillion-dollar global conglomerate.

You probably know a few people you work with whom you would describe with one or two words that speak to their greatest and most visible strength.

In our work within an array of companies and firms, we have encountered:

- **The Fixer**—He's the go-to guru who can make anything better.
- **The Simplifier**—She's the "bottom-line-it for me" champ.
- **The Innovator**—She's the "big audacious ideas" generator.
- **The Whiz Kid**—He's the talented Gen Y hire on rocket fuel.
- **The Rock**—He's the "we'll get it done" calm port in the storm.
- **The Organizer**—She's the project manager extraordinaire.
- **The Mediator**—He's the "no one walks away angry" team player.

- **The Negotiator**—She's the tough-as-nails, win-win producer.
- **The Connector**—He's the networker who always knows someone you should know.
- **The Sales Star**—He's the guy who never met a sales challenge he didn't love.
- **The Guru**—She's the oracle who's happy to share her knowledge.
- **The Juggler**—She's the one who keeps all the balls in the air and doesn't drop one—ever!

How many people do you encounter who can be defined by a word or two? We meet them all the time as we coach executives through identifying and building strong personal brands. Deb worked with a client who was known as "Mr. One-Pager." He was adept at simplifying advanced concepts and would condense his annual plan from a slide deck into a single slide. That one clear slide became his team's road map. The road map's simplicity fostered innovation by allowing the team to detour, get creative, and test things out, yet remain focused on the goal because it was so easy to get back on course.

What's *your* word or phrase? Think about which of your greatest strengths can propel you to the top of your profession. Make a plan to integrate that single strength into everything you do, every day. You'll become known for it.

What do you want to be known for?

DO | Identify THE strength you want to be known for. Then look at everything you do each week and refine how you do it to maximize your strength. You'll be in a class by yourself. You'll be memorable.

Branding Is about Emotion: Be Loved

Emotion is *not* touchy-feely. It's good branding and good business!

"The best CEOs are truly 'Chief Emotions Officers,' since great companies have great cultures, and at the heart of a great culture are healthy emotions. You may not think of yourself as a leader, but you are already leading yourself—and maybe others—on a daily basis." So says CEO Chip Conley in his book *Emotional Equations*.

Emotion is all around you. Conley knows it, we know it, and so do you. You know people in your company who just exude attractive qualities that get people using the "L" word when they describe them.

*We **love** Ellen; she is so full of energy and optimism.*

*I **love** Jose; he always tells it like it is.*

Emotion is an essential component of branding, and being loved means creating an emotional bond through the recognition of your attractive qualities. Developing emotional bonds with your constituents ensures that they connect with you, even if they don't agree with everything you do.

In his book *Love Is the Killer App*, bestselling author Tim Sanders calls this being a Lovecat—a nice, smart person who succeeds at business and in life.

Strongly branded executives aren't afraid to get emotional! They succeed by radiating emotional brand attributes, not merely those that are rational (you can read about both types in Chapter 5, Snap 2, "Be Competent"). Their authenticity attracts connection, love, and loyalty.

Allowing yourself to exude emotion—to be loved—is freeing, fun, and just makes life and work better.

Creating emotional connections means first being yourself—exuding those attributes that enable connection. And sometimes that feels hard, and may even feel off-brand. We know of a hard-working career coach who is a "big hugger." If you see her at a coaching association meeting, she'll likely be in an embrace with someone or at least have an arm around a shoulder.

She told us that she wasn't happy with being known as the caring coach. She wanted to be known as the expert coach, or the visionary coach, or the wildly successful coach, but *not* the caring coach. That was until she realized that her caring nature *was* her brand differentiator. She *really* cared about her clients, about the coaching profession, and about the world around her. People consistently saw it in what she did and how she did it. She was expert, she was visionary, and she was wildly successful, but her secret ingredient—the ingredient that enabled all of those things—was her innate caring nature, and her willingness to wear it on her sleeve.

Would people use the "L" word to describe you? Are you ready to become a Chief Emotions Officer?

DARE

Get emotional! Don't be afraid. Strong brands build loyal mega-fan clubs by creating enduring, authentic, emotional connections. Smile—you *can* do this! You can even love doing it!

My Sparks

Record your ideas, sparked from Chapter 3.

Chapter Four

KNOW

Be Grounded

Know and Live Your Values

Have a Vision

Have a Mission

Be in Alignment:

Know and Live Your Values

Values are your standard operating procedures.

Values are the principles that are most important to you. They may be part of your moral code, or they may be the guiding force for how you prefer to do things. They are your way of *being*.

Knowing your values is important; living them is critical. When you, or others, violate your values, you may become frustrated, ashamed, and even angry. But when your values are in alignment, friction is removed. Energy is restored. You are able to stay on track and build momentum.

William had a client who woke early to get to work while his kids were still sleeping and often returned home to find them already in their beds. He thought he hated his job, but, in fact, he just didn't like violating his number one value—family. So he made a change. Once a week, every week, he went home for lunch and spent time with his wife and kids. He didn't mind the extra commuting time and found he actually *did* like his job. He also realized that he had more control than he was giving himself. He realized his schedule was not imposed upon him. He had a choice—and he decided to align his approach to work with his most important value. Not only was he was more fulfilled, he was better at his job.

Peace was likely Dr. Martin Luther King Jr.'s top value; it was evident in everything he did. Peaceful protest was his approach to accomplishing true equality for African Americans in the United States. While many of his contemporaries promoted change through violent unrest, Dr. King stood fast for the power of non-violence, creating an iconic movement that forever changed the landscape of race relations in America.

Being that clear about your values helps you understand your connection to the values of your team, organization, and company. Understanding your common values will help you feel better about the company you work for and enable you to confidently deliver on the company's brand promise.

William's top value is optimism. Deb's top value is connection. Do you know yours? Values are important to you as a leader—leaders use values to build, inspire, and engage their teams. Richard Branson's value of risk-taking, Steve Job's value of innovation, and Starbucks' Howard Schultz's value of community are clearly evident in the organizations they built.

Are you living and working in alignment with your values?

DITCH | Switch off the cruise control. Stop. Really look at yourself. What are your top values? Are you living them every day? If not, press reset and get on course!

Be Connected to the World:

Have a Vision

Your vision is what you see as possible for the world.

How often do you spend time thinking about a change you would like to see happen in the world?

This sounds really lofty. Most of us rarely think about such huge topics; we focus great amounts of time on things that are more mundane and routine.

Yet, all strong brands have some connection to an audacious goal. Bill and Melinda Gates want to bring education to people everywhere in the world. British chef Jamie Oliver sees the kitchen as a place to give everyone a start at a career. Bruce Springsteen hopes to spur action by shining a light on the problems of working-class people and failed political agendas.

You don't have to be a billionaire, renowned chef, or celebrity to have a global vision. You probably know people in your life and workplace who are involved in causes that fulfill their need to make a difference—and you remember them, because in a world of multitasking and self-absorption, vision is a differentiator. Vision, and the energetic positivity it engenders, makes you memorable within your brand community, whether you are working quietly behind the scenes or on the world's stage.

People with a vision have a charisma that comes from conviction and confidence. Vision gives even the quietest people rare courage—courage that is compelling and respected. It doesn't matter whether their vision is popular; the fact that they hold to it, work toward it, and authentically live it is what draws people to them and makes them memorable.

William's vision is a world where everyone has the opportunity to reach his or her full potential through personal branding. That's why he calls his company Reach Personal Branding.

Deb's vision is a world where innovative leaders who blend a strong profit motive with a social conscience become the go-to change agents for "capitalism done right." She has built her brand around that vision—and that attracts the innovators and world changers with whom she loves to work.

Vision doesn't happen in distraction. Slow down a bit and take some time to think of the ideal world you'd like to see, of the legacy you'd like to leave. Like Bill and Melinda, Jamie, Bruce, and countless other visionaries, get in touch with the cause that touches *you*. Then figure out how you can make a difference.

What do YOU think is possible for the world?

DARE

Stop multitasking for a moment. Spend time thinking. What do you feel are the greatest injustices in the world? What important issues affect you emotionally? People care about people who care!

Live Your Purpose:
Have a Mission

Your *mission* is your contribution to making your *vision* a reality.

Having a vision is great, but without purpose, a vision remains no more than a lovely idea. Purpose guides your efforts, and your efforts can have a huge impact as you inspire others to join in your mission. In fact, you often *need* to inspire others to accomplish your mission.

Bill and Melinda Gates are not going to change literacy and education by themselves, but they are rallying social scientists, educators, innovators, and others to their cause. Jamie Oliver's visibility, through his books and TV appearances, has been able to mobilize others to support his vision of giving everyone—especially troubled and underprivileged youth—the opportunity to launch a career. Bruce Springsteen carries on the traditions of Woodie Guthrie and Pete Seeger with powerful anthems that entertain while rousing legions of fans to consider the need for social change.

William's mission is to use the power of personal branding to inspire people to act on their own dreams and soar. He built his personal branding certification program to get coaches involved so he could amplify his impact.

Deb's mission is to propel innovative, ethical, "profit and people" executives to positions of greater influence so they can change the world. She supports her values by working with clients who share those values and mission.

The bonus? Both Deb and William love their work and feel a deep and satisfying commitment to their clients.

Companies are realizing that embracing a mission is good business. Today, customers and employees want to connect with something bigger and "nobler" than they are as individuals—they want to tap into the power of a collective vision and mission.

Companies that have a clear and authentic mission build loyal customers and stakeholders who feel invested in that mission. As a strong personal brand with a clear mission, you can attract like-minded loyal fans, too.

Mahatma Gandhi remarked, "If we could change ourselves, the tendencies in the world would also change. As a man changes his own nature, so does the attitude of the world change towards him. ...We need not wait to see what others do."

Pursue *your* vision and mission! Once you establish your purpose and connect it with what you do, you will inspire others and feel an incredible sense of accomplishment and connection.

How can you help make your vision a reality?

DITCH

Stop believing you can't make a difference. You can! Start turning your vision into a real mission! When you believe you can make a difference, you will—and you'll inspire others to help.

My Sparks

Record your ideas, sparked from Chapter 4.

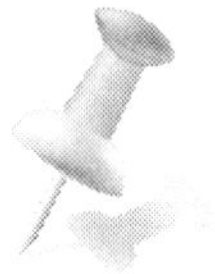

Chapter Five

KNOW

Be Relevant

Be Open

Be Competent

Contribute a Unique Ingredient

Feedback Counts:

Be Open

Professional success doesn't happen in a vacuum.

Self-awareness is essential to building your executive brand. But in branding, it's not only what *you* think that matters. Your brand is held in the hearts and minds of those around you—your team, clients, colleagues, managers, friends, and family.

You *need* honest input—about what you do *and* about who you are. Sadly, the higher you move in the company, the more you hear what others *think* you want to hear—and the less you hear about what you *really* need to know.

Actively seek truthful input. Some of it may be uncomfortable, but it's a critical and lifelong part of building and propelling your brand. And it's never too early to start. Back in ancient times—when Deb was a friendly, impressionable, twentysomething in her first real job—she was trained by an aloof boss who believed that professionalism equaled an emotionless team with no collegial friendships. The culture was suffocating, and, in time, Deb left for a new company. She excelled in her duties but was shocked to receive a poor review. Her new boss said her inability to connect with others was hurting her performance and jeopardizing her position. Deb hadn't realized how deeply she'd been imprinted with the toxic ideas of her previous boss.

Deb found the feedback painful and embarrassing, but it was also a huge relief to know that she could bring her authentic self to work. She became known throughout the organization, was promoted, and made good friends on the job (including her future husband!). Deb's experience taught her an early and enduring lesson in seeking feedback.

Strong brands are *obsessive* about obtaining honest input. Integrate opportunities to receive feedback into every aspect of your job. Get real-time feedback from your team. Call a client after a meeting to get his thoughts on how it went. Ask your manager what she considers to be your greatest strengths and best opportunities for development. Validate feedback from different sources to gain clarity on external perceptions.

When William founded Reach Personal Branding, there was no way to get candid anonymous feedback about someone's brand. So he developed a revolutionary program, 360Reach, to help people understand their reputation from the outside in, because even one clear insight from the outside world can forever change the course of a career.

Here's one example. William knew a VP of finance who received a comment in her 360Reach feedback that said, "I don't understand why you're in finance; you seem like a marketer to me." It touched a nerve; she'd always wanted to be in marketing, but her career took off in finance and before she knew it, she was a VP. That one statement inspired her to transfer to marketing (in a less senior role). She's now a VP in marketing and couldn't be happier.

Don't wait for these valuable "outside-in" insights to magically appear. Seek them, welcome them, and use them!

Do you know what people think about you?

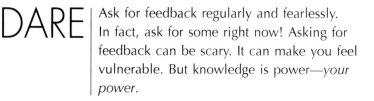

DARE | Ask for feedback regularly and fearlessly. In fact, ask for some right now! Asking for feedback can be scary. It can make you feel vulnerable. But knowledge is power—*your power*.

Get in the Game:

Be Competent

Competence is key to successful personal branding.

Competence gets you into the game. It's your *minimum* eligibility requirement. It's the combination of skills essential to do the job at hand.

Competence isn't sexy, but it *is* essential. No matter how interesting, attractive, or compelling you are, you won't be considered for a particular role if you can't meet the specs.

Continually work on the skills necessary to perform your job. Are your leadership skills up to snuff? Do your communication skills get people to listen? Do you possess the technical skills required for your role?

If you don't have the skills to do your job, all the emotion in the world won't endear you to the people who are making decisions about you.

Continuous professional development is core to any strong brand. According to futurist Ray Kurzweil, knowledge doubles every year. Brand-savvy lifelong learners build actionable development plans to stay current and relevant with new knowledge.

If you're not learning something new but think that's okay because you know your job, we say, with respect, "You're delusional!" You're not maintaining; you're falling behind, because the minimum requirements for competency keep increasing as the world of work evolves.

For example, just a few years ago, these innovations were barely on the radar for most executives. Now…

- Social media savvy has become a minimum requirement for nearly every job.
- Running a virtual team meeting is an essential skill.
- Crowdsourcing impacts every company function, from product development to marketing, from corporate events to CEO communications.
- Video is transforming the way we communicate and build personal brands with our internal and external stakeholders.
- A branded presence on Google and LinkedIn has quickly become a requirement for online professional presence.

Competence alone won't take you to the finish line, but without it, you won't even make the starting gate. Standing still means you're already behind. Today's major competency requirement may simply be managing the evolution required by the revolution.

What are the minimum eligibility requirements for your next role?

DO | Rate your proficiency in the skills required for your ideal next role. Make note of gaps. Create a development plan to eliminate them. Then do it!

Conformity Is the Enemy of Innovation:

Contribute a Unique Ingredient

Innovate and differentiate to remain successful.

In the world of branding, your job title is as much a commodity as coffee beans, pork bellies, or crude oil.

Chances are that there are others at your company or firm who share your job title. And there are many more people with the same job title in companies all over the world. If what *you* offer is the same as what *they* offer, you have no competitive advantage. You will always be in contention with the person who will do the work for the least pay.

At the commodity level, one bushel of coffee beans is interchangeable with another. One person doing a job is interchangeable with another. The market sets the price.

However, when you are a brand, you are premium quality. You are Starbucks coffee. We pay a premium for Starbucks coffee because the taste and the experience are not available anywhere else. Your company pays a premium for you because only you deliver what the company needs.

True innovation comes from creativity and diversity—from each employee delivering a unique ingredient that's not available from anyone else.

Of course, having a unique and valuable skill set can be the clear differentiation you need to be considered a premium product. Or, rather than a skill set, your unique ingredient might be as simple as the enthusiasm you bring to work, or the way you bring out the best in your team, or even the whimsy of your office or cube décor.

The ability to pair a unique skill *and* an emotional connection to stakeholders can be a true critical advantage. Deb has a friend whose mom continued working well past retirement age. She was a quality control professional loved by all and affectionately known as "Ms. Eagle Eyes." Her record of catching imperfections was legendary. At a time when manufacturers were laying off legions of staff and executives, Ms. Eagle Eyes was always safe. "Please don't retire; please give us another year. We can't lose you!" was the annual refrain. That's what unique ingredients can do.

Fashion design is a very competitive field, but the late Alexander McQueen was able to carve out his place by offering something unique: the combination of strong design elements with delicate fabrics. If what *you* can contribute is valued and is available only from you and not from your peers, you are differentiated and valuable. You create demand for your services. You are in a class by yourself. You have control of your career.

What's your unique ingredient?

DO

Take inventory. What qualities deliver value and make you unique among your peers? Use them to make your greatest contribution to corporate innovation and career momentum.

My Sparks

Record your ideas, sparked from Chapter 5.

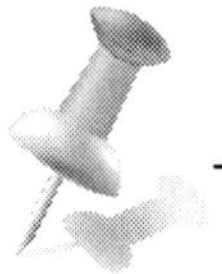

Chapter Six | Be Courageous

KNOW

Be Fearless

Fail Frequently

Be Opinionated

Step Outside Your Comfort Zone:
Be Fearless

Fear is a perpetual red light.

Sometimes fear is good. If you are walking alone down a dark alley at night, fear will keep you alert. However, in your career, fear can hold you back. Risk-taking is part of branding because strong brands aren't satisfied with the status quo; they live to grow.

Do you want to be known for what you avoided—or for what you faced?

From time to time, even the most successful leaders can become paralyzed, or at least "slowed down," by fear. Once they are able to look at the situation that prompted the fear, view it through a different lens, and face the challenge, they eagerly greet new opportunities.

Fear can prevent you from making a networking connection or asking a high-profile colleague for help. It can impact a meeting with a prospective client or stop you from pursuing a position that you would really like to have. Fear impedes success, and, even more importantly, fear breeds more fear. The more you fear, the worse the fear becomes.

Our colleague, Petek Kabakci, doesn't let fear hold her back. She told us, "I am an introvert. I prefer to read, observe, and think, not to talk. If I talk, I use few words and get right to the point. My long-term goal is to be a thought leader, a recognized coach and consultant. My logical, objective side encouraged me to step far outside my comfort zone and do what is needed to accomplish my goals. So I arranged to host a local conference on personal branding—not something an introvert would naturally do. A TV channel heard about it and requested an interview, and in the spirit of greeting new challenges, I accepted—and stepped into a new arena with no option of turning back."

We all know the absolute rush of relief and pride we feel after accomplishing something big that we dreaded and avoided—and we can say, "That wasn't so bad!"

This book is filled with opportunities to step outside your comfort zone—they are the "dares" in *Ditch. Dare. Do!*—and there are likely dozens, even hundreds, of dares you will think of and encounter over the course of your career.

Start now. It's time to venture outside of what is safe and comfortable and secure. Bestselling author and business guru Seth Godin says, "Playing safe is very risky." We agree.

Are you ready to face your fears?

DITCH | Replace the word "fear" with "fabulous!" Greet challenges as rich opportunities—fantastic new ways to shine, grow, and demonstrate your greatness!

Success Comes from Failure:

Fail Frequently

If you never fail, you aren't taking enough risks.

Without risk, you don't grow or stretch yourself. Without growth, you stagnate, while those around you move ahead. Fear of failure often prevents action, yet failing is the catalyst for growth and success.

When you fail (notice we didn't say "if"), you'll be joining a long list of iconic business leaders, scientists, authors, athletes, educators, and celebrity "failures." Albert Einstein was speech and reading delayed as a child, and later expelled from school. Henry Ford experienced multiple business failures. Thomas Edison developed more than 1,000 failed prototypes of the first electric lightbulb.

During his first stand-up gig, Jerry Seinfeld was booed off the stage. "Become a secretary," suggested Marilyn Monroe's first modeling agents. Stephen King received 30 rejections when submitting his first book, the iconic thriller *Carrie*. A young Elvis Presley was fired by the Grand Ole Opry's manager after one performance and advised to go back to driving a truck.

What's your current risk quotient? Do you run from projects that have risk written all over them? Are you the first to sign up for "cake-walk" projects? Avoiding risk is a good strategy for short-term wins, but it won't prepare you for success in the future. Caution will impede growth.

Accept jobs that come with some risk. If you take on only those assignments or positions where you are guaranteed success, you are missing opportunities to learn, grow, and impress. And you are missing the chance to showcase your brand attribute of "fearless."

Take inventory of events that you classified as failures and look for the growth that came from them. Many of them are likely the foundation for some of your most powerful successes. This should be all you need to convince yourself of the power and benefits of failure.

Highlighting your failures during a client meeting with your manager or with your team can be powerful. Let your manager know that you are motivated to take calculated risks and are willing to fail if it means growing professionally and moving forward. And encourage your team to take calculated risks. It's good for them and good for the success of your organization.

In *The Adventures of Johnny Bunko: The Last Career Guide You'll Ever Need,* author Dan Pink says, "The most successful people make spectacular mistakes—huge, honking screw ups! Why? They're trying to do something big. But each time they make a mistake, they get a little better and move a little closer to excellence."

Do you have the courage to make a spectacular, huge, honking screw up?

DARE

Wrestle risk and "fail forward!" Classify your current projects' risk level. If all your projects are low risk, sign on for some higher-risk opportunities. Chances are, failing forward will accelerate your career.

Get Off the Fence:

Be Opinionated

Wishy-washy people can only go so far.

Neutrality is for diplomats. Unless your career goal is to be the ambassador to the UN, get on your soapbox! Trying to please all of the people all of the time is a recipe for frustration and mediocrity.

Take a position. It's not about being contrary; it's about having a point of view that reflects your convictions. It's about being able to powerfully articulate and express your beliefs.

Strong brands often repel as many people as they attract. And that's okay.

Look at Russell Brand, Donald Trump, Sarah Palin, Snooki, Ricky Gervais, Rachel Maddow, Chelsea Handler, Bill O'Reilly, Charlie Sheen, Perez Hilton, and Lady Gaga. Each has enthusiastic supporters and fervent detractors. Each is willing to courageously stand up for his or her beliefs and stand out from the undecided masses. When you clearly, confidently, and consistently express your point of view, you'll attract those who share your beliefs. And those who don't share them will often respect them.

When Deb was a student in the personal branding certification program, she was really stuck in describing her target audience. For many of her peers in the program, demographics guided their choice of client niche—but the demographics of age, job title, or industry couldn't define the group of people with whom Deb loves to work. She enjoys working with a type of executive who is gutsy, visionary, innovative, fun, irreverent, and ethical—the type of executive who, Deb says, lives by "capitalism done right."

Focusing on what seems like a small group of people was scary to Deb. Her description of her ideal client rules out most people. It took guts to own it and a huge amount of courage to be overt in communicating this to the world. And that's exactly what Deb has done. Her website prominently describes her ideal client, and if you call her office phone, her voicemail message discourages all non-ideal clients yet confirms that she is the right coach for those people with whom she loves to work.

Like Deb, be opinionated! If you're the marketing executive who believes advertising is all about creativity—trying new things—own it. And be willing to debate your marketing colleagues who believe advertising is about metrics.

Leaders who exude their convictions through all that they do gain respect and visibility. They become mega brands—almost larger than life—and the default leaders for their causes.

What are your convictions?

DARE | Take a stand—have a platform. Strong opinions are foundational to all mega brands, and they feel good, too. Being opinionated is power branding!

My Sparks

Record your ideas, sparked from Chapter 6.

Chapter Seven

KNOW

Be Deliberate

Be Consistent

Make Your Mark

Remain Relevant

Deliver on Your Promise:
Be Consistent

Consistency builds a strong reputation.

Strong brands don't change their promise of value; they demonstrate it through all that they do. Consistency is core to every strong brand. This important thread links all of the world's most successful brands.

Oprah is consistent in her brand message. No matter what she does in her media empire, the thing people remember most about her is her empathy. As a talk show host, when her peers were exploiting their guests, she was hugging hers. When she ventured into reality TV, she launched "The Big Give," which combined reality with philanthropy. Her empathy for victims of distracted drivers led her to start the "No Phone Zone" pledge drive. She founded and built the OWN cable network to continue helping people improve their lives and the lives of others.

You can see that everything Oprah does is consistent with her foundational brand of empathy. If she were cold and distant, her fans would feel confused and even betrayed. Her brand would lose its luster.

And even though OWN was struggling at the time this book was written, Oprah's brand has not faded; rather, her risk-taking has endeared her to her fans. It's likely that her steadfast commitment to helping people improve their circumstances, ability to rally the right resources to make things happen, and authentic connection to her fan base will get OWN on the right track.

William knows a woman whose brand is all about creativity. She works for an IT company and is such a believer in the power of creativity to solve problems and engage people that she deliberately and consistently integrates creativity into everything she does. The agendas for her meetings are crossword puzzles in which attendees have to guess the agenda topics. She invites the whole office to quarterly creative brainstorming workshops and has a "creativity" wall in her office with images and words of inspiration that help her maintain her creative edge.

Consistency is just as important for you. What's *your* differentiation? What makes *you* exceptional? Are you demonstrating these things and how they create value every day, with everything you do?

If you send incompatible messages, those around you will not know what you stand for *or* what to expect from you. Steadfastly communicating *your* unique promise of value through all that you do enables you to greatly expand *your* success.

How consistent is YOUR reputation?

DO | Strive for consistency in every human touch point—in every interaction you have with others. Consistency builds trust; trust builds brands. Period.

Contribute with Everything You Do:

Make Your Mark

Great brands don't just show up; they stand out.

Great brands bring their A-game, every day. They carry out their brand promise. They know that meeting their mandate to deliver value in everything they do isn't showing off; it's fulfilling a brand covenant made with their company at hire. And in a culture of ever-increasing distraction, keeping that covenant is a hard-won victory—as anyone who has tried to communicate with a preoccupied multitasker can attest.

In an ideal world, you'd focus 100% of your attention on the task at hand. Yet today's frenetic workplace almost demands a level of distraction just to get things done. According to Gen Y filmmaker, futurist, and self-proclaimed "wonder junkie" Jason Silva, "Attention is the new scarce resource."

We've all experienced the frustration of multitasker communication (or been guilty of it) at a meeting (yes, we do notice that your notes look like email!), on the phone (do you really think we don't know you're typing?), or even in person (we see you texting under the desk, and we're offended).

The difference between distracted (and distracting) multitaskers and strong brands is this: Strong brands don't fight distraction with attention; they *meet distraction with intention*. Intention means knowing how and what you want to contribute so you don't miss opportunities to make your mark—to express and leverage your brand on a daily basis. If you've attended your meeting but were working on the report that's overdue rather than actively contributing and leaving your mark, have you done your job? When you check your email while on a teleconference or text under the table in the middle of a client meeting, have you missed an opportunity to build your brand?

We know an executive who manages every interaction with intention. He arrives at work 90 minutes early, using that uninterrupted time to strategize new initiatives, review projects, prioritize needed actions, write necessary emails, and assign tasks. When the rest of the team arrives, it's go time. They've got their marching orders, and he's in full execution mode, with full attention.

From his earliest days with the organization, he has been known as the big idea guy who can make it happen no matter what. When the position he held was nearly eliminated in an organization-wide reengineering, he was one of just two executives chosen to continue in that role, while his counterparts were laid off or reassigned. The seeds of value, when sown, grow deep roots.

Strong brands like this executive aren't content to go through the motions. They see every call, client interaction, and team meeting as an opportunity to strengthen their team, their organization, *and* their career.

They don't just show up. Do you?

DITCH | Starting today, look at every item on your calendar. Decide in advance, with intention, how to transform them into (or replace them with) brand-building activities that will help you stand out (and pay attention).

Strong Brands Evolve:

Remain Relevant

In life, change is the only constant, and it's accelerating.

Strong brands understand that change and evolution transform the workplace every day. Evolution takes what worked in the past and replaces it with change that works for the future. Strong brands are willing—even eager—to pioneer the evolution that continued success demands.

Be ever aware of what's happening around you and consider this wisdom from GE's legendary Jack Welch: "If the rate of change on the outside exceeds the rate of change on the inside, the end is near." Develop the new competencies that change requires—the new ways your evolving brand can create value. Be a lifelong learner; develop new, appropriate skills; and understand which parts of your brand are going to be most compelling to the future of your team and organization.

Social media is just one example of an evolutionary change that has become a required skill that creates new value. Even if social media isn't your job, it's a tool you can use to be more successful *at* your job. If you're in HR, social media provides a new way to source candidates. If you're in IT, it's a way to get a technical challenge solved. Social media breaks down barriers to expert minds that traditional methods could never reach. Those who have embraced it as a work tool are set apart from their more change-resistant peers.

Another evolutionary change is the four-generation workplace. With the retirement age lengthening, companies find themselves with a workforce of Boomers, Gen X-ers, Gen Y "Nexters," and even some indispensable "Veteran" stalwarts. Strong brands not only consider how to function in this multigenerational environment but how to use it to their advantage.

Deb knows a Boomer executive recognized as a de facto talent incubator for his organization—the go-to developer of young hires. He treats his interns and emerging professionals as valued employees, coaching them, assigning them important responsibilities, and giving them ownership of projects. They are key team members and proud of it. His fun (he's always up on the latest in technology, music, and popular culture) yet tough development style brings out their best and then makes their best better. When they move on to new roles, they're ready to hit the ground running and move up quickly. And the company values him for that.

Weak brands are relics, reluctant to change until change demands action. Strong brands are perpetual, relevant pioneers who fearlessly embrace change, create change, and promote change. And in turn, change promotes them!

Are you a reluctant relic or a relevant change agent?

DARE | Evolve fearlessly! Strong brands evolve, remaining uniquely relevant and valuable, no matter what change throws at them. Their resilience opens them to opportunities.

My Sparks

Record your ideas, sparked from Chapter 7.

Chapter Eight | Be Whole

KNOW

Rise to the Top

Chill!

Start Blending

Be in Top Form:
Rise to the Top

Good health is a professional priority.

Being healthy won't get you to your goals, but poor health, low energy, and bad eating habits will certainly impede your professional success.

Regardless of your industry or role, work takes mental and physical energy. Brands are built on a solid foundation of physical health. That means eating right, moving your body, and getting the sleep you need. This sounds obvious, yet most of us could do a little (or a lot) more to manage our health.

Do you eat things you would normally avoid just because it's convenient? Do you wake up most mornings feeling like you could use a few more hours of shut-eye? Do you find yourself skipping the gym so you can reduce your email backlog?

If you answered yes to any of these questions, you're missing an opportunity to perform at your physical peak. And you're establishing habits that will impact your ability to achieve your goals.

Luanne Tierney, VP of Worldwide Partner Marketing at Juniper Networks, says, "Physical fitness is not just something I do to stay healthy, it's part of my brand. I get my best ideas while working out and listening to music. Everyone knows I am at the gym every morning early—weight training or even swimming laps. Making health a priority helps me stand out while giving me the energy and stamina I need to maintain while working in the fast-paced world of high tech! Having a fit mindset and body gives me a total edge at work and is a huge confidence booster."

Beth Stefani, executive career coach and founder of Inspire Careers Inc., stresses that true health demands an open and observant mind. Beth says, "I believe that we need to find joy in all of the little things that happen every day in our lives. If we want to experience joy right now, all we need to do is open our eyes and take time to see the beauty around us." When was the last time you stopped multitasking, really lived in the moment, and took joy in the little things? Try it! In fact, practice doing it every day. Experiencing joy is a healthy habit!

According to a Continuum Care Alliance survey, 84% of employers and health plans across the United States have a wellness program. They offer these programs because the financial savings gained from healthy employees make it good business. And they know that healthy employees are productive employees. It's good for your brand if you participate. Many employees don't. Do you?

What can you do to increase your physical health?

DARE | Get healthy NOW! Join a gym. Run before work or take a walk at lunch. Replace pastrami-on-rye with a salad. Turn off your laptop before midnight. You can do it, and you can like it!

Don't Be Defined by Stress: Chill!

Your value is *not* directly proportional to your level of stress.

Stress case. Is that the label you want to wear in front of those who are making decisions about you? Is that how you want your teams to see you? It's true that stress is an inevitable part of work. In fact, the "Attitudes in the American Workplace VI" Gallup Poll found that 80% of workers feel stress on the job. How you deal with that stress, *if* you deal with that stress, is something under your control.

Are you running around the office with your hair on fire? Is the stress of work making you behave in ways that are not consistent with who you are and how you want to be known? A little adrenalin is a good thing; it keeps you on your toes. But don't let a pump of adrenalin become a flood of unmanaged daily insanity. When you're that stressed, you stop being you; you become the person people avoid or complain about. And that's not good branding!

Lou Holtz, renowned football coach, said, "It's not the load that breaks you down, it's the way you carry it." Professional athletes work all year to be in perfect physical form; if you want a strong brand, you need to be as focused as an athlete in reducing stress, so you can radiate your true brand attributes.

Deb worked with "Juliet," a high-powered, make-it-happen-yesterday executive and working mother, who was scattered and stressed and making her teams stressed, too. Juliet was delivering what workplace stress expert Jordan Friedman, aka the Stress Coach, calls "secondhand stress." According to Friedman, secondhand stress " ...impacts you and those around you and it's hazardous to your brand. Stress shuts down two-way communication, hinders problem solving, and sends an 'I'm more important than you' message. It repels instead of attracts."

Juliet worked on reframing her stressful situations and creating a calming environment. An avid photographer and music lover, she filled her office with her collection of sunrise photographs, a small fountain, comfy chairs, and a collection of music ranging from upbeat to chill. It became a productive environment in which she (and her teams) could relax, recharge, and refocus. Productivity soared, and everyone had more fun at work.

Know your stress triggers, and know what type of stress reduction works best for you. Friedman says, and we agree, "Stress impacts performance and job satisfaction. Knowing how to recognize and manage your stress is the single most valuable leadership skill you can master."

Are you proud that "stressed out" is one of your brand attributes? Are you willin' to be chillin'?

DITCH | Stop wearing stress as a badge of honor! Stop thinking stress is uncontrollable. Yes, we're talking to YOU! Managing stress is good for you, your teams, and your company.

Stop Balancing:
Start Blending

It's not work vs. life. It's just life.

Self-help gurus, life coaches, and the media extol the benefits of seemingly achievable work-life equilibrium. And before the Internet, smartphones, laptops, iPads, and globalization, the concept of work-life balance was believable.

Today, if you constantly seek the nirvana of work-life balance, you will experience work and life as battling entities. You'll feel guilty when returning phone calls after normal business hours. You'll wonder if you are spending enough time on work. You'll regret checking your email on vacation. "Balance" will equal "stress." Instead, think of work as a part of life and integrate who you are into what you do. Decide when and where you work. Choose how to blend, not balance.

If you think your company won't be on board, ask. You might be surprised. Companies increasingly understand the blurring of business and personal. If the company is okay with you picking up your kids from school or volunteering at a literacy center for an hour during your business day, you'll be less likely to resent finishing up a project at night. "I have made it a priority to make work and life fit together," said Mary Gorges, a communications director at Cisco. "I am a devoted single mom and a serious professional who's passionate about storytelling. I have felt intuitively that I can't let my work life compete with taking care of my son and don't want my family commitments to negatively impact my career. So, I am clear with everyone in my life about the importance of both."

Penelope Trunk, author of *Brazen Careerist: The New Rules of Success*, wrote in a 2007 blog post, "The lines between work and life have been blurred for years. I have decided to embrace this fact and work on the best blend for my life. Whether this means working hours that fit around my schedule or being paid for results rather than the amount of hours worked, I'm not sure. I will leave that question to the management consultants and human resource experts. In the meantime, my peers and I will keep searching for this blended life, while everyone else continues to run in circles failing to achieve their so-called balance."

In the five years between 2008 and 2013 (the year of this book's completion), the explosion of smartphones, iPads, and ubiquitous video conferencing has virtually erased the final barriers that separated work and life. It's time to surrender, adapt, and embrace the blend. Because today, the more you fight bringing who you are into work and work into who you are, the more tension, dissatisfaction, frustration, and guilt you will encounter.

Are you ready to stop fighting the work vs. life battle?

DARE | Give yourself permission—no, a mandate—to replace the "work you" and "life you" with just "you." An authentic whole life feels GOOD!

My Sparks

Record your ideas, sparked from Chapter 8.

My KNOW

Go-time Grid

Learning has little value without action!

Go back to the ditch, dare, and do sparks that you documented after each chapter in KNOW. Break them into tasks you can put on your "do-list." Use the table below to describe the task, assign it a priority, and note the date by which you will complete it.

You can document your thoughts here, or download the PDF version of this chart at ditchdaredo.com/resources.

Ditch, Dare, or Do	Priority	Concrete action I will take	What do I want to achieve from it?	Date

Ditch, Dare, or Do	Priority	Concrete action I will take	What do I want to achieve from it?	Date

amazon.com

A gift note from Cindy Key:

Lisa, Hope you will both enjoy Ditch Dare Do & it will help you be more successful. All the best, Cindy Key, Key Concepts www.AccelerateYourSearch.com

Gift note included with **Ditch, Dare, Do: 3D Personal Branding for Executives**

SHOW

Tell It to Sell It!

Quick Quiz

Who Are You Talking To?

What's Your Message?

How Do You Say It?

How Do You Document It?

How Do You Package Your Message?

How Do You Package Your World?

Show Your Brand:

Tell It to Sell It!

You've discovered your brand. Now you know who you are! Exciting! It's time to show *the world* who you are. It's time to tell your story.

Strong brands are constantly evolving narratives of interesting, expert, relevant value that build market presence, create excitement, and attract opportunities. Strong brands are stories. And their stories transform facts into a good read—powerful, memorable, and actionable. They tell employers, leaders, teams, and customers what they want to know.

As an executive, you may be skeptical about "telling a story." If so, listen to the experts. In his book *A Whole New Mind,* author Daniel Pink identifies "Story" as one of the six aptitudes central to success and satisfaction. Gary Vaynerchuck, the author of *Crush It!,* asserts, "Storytelling is by far the most underrated skill in business." Howard Gardner of Harvard University says that "stories are the single most powerful weapon in a leader's arsenal."

But before you toot your own horn, you'll need to write the score. You'll need to be clear about what your brand community needs so you can use that information as a filter to craft a story that truly speaks to your brand community's desires. Be sure to weave in who you are and the passions you hold. You'll have an authentic, relevant, and compelling narrative.

In Part Two, SHOW, you'll answer six questions designed to help you craft your authentic story and relate your relevant value:

1. Who are you talking to?
2. What's your message?
3. How do you say it?
4. How do you document it?
5. How do you package your message?
6. How do you package your world?

By the end of Part Two, you'll have told your story. In doing so, you will have defined your brand community, created your Why-Buy-ROI branded value message, dumped your boring resume, and developed a suite of branded career marketing materials and storied accomplishment scripts that will help you open doors to partners or clients, get promoted, or land your ideal job.

We encourage you to make storytelling the foundation of your brand communications. Develop strong narrative skills and you'll propel your career.

QUICK QUIZ

Before you dive into SHOW, rate how well you show up!

Rate how you show up!				
Strongly Disagree				**Strongly Agree**
I have defined and identified the people who need to know me so I can reach my goals.				
1	2	3	4	5
I actively spend time with my team and colleagues every week.				
1	2	3	4	5
I have a 15-second value pitch that expresses my brand and attracts the right people.				
1	2	3	4	5
I have a library of success stories I use to demonstrate my branded value.				
1	2	3	4	5
My bio reflects the true me and is compelling to people who are making decisions about me.				
1	2	3	4	5
I know my brand color and consistently use it in my personal communications.				
1	2	3	4	5
My office/environment communicates who I am and/or what is unique about me (interests, strengths, etc.).				
1	2	3	4	5

Total: ______

Now, add up your score. How close did you come to 35? Working through this section—SHOW—will help you make your brand message clear, consistent, and compelling. What are you waiting for?

Chapter Nine

SHOW

Who Are You Talking To?

Inspire Your Team!

Brand Within

Be Seen

Be a Leader:

Inspire Your Team!

Your team looks to you for more than job assignments.

Your team wants a trusted role model, mentor, and advocate—a leader with whom they can be productive and grow.

Just as with corporate brands, your executive brand holds an inspirational promise of value. It separates you from your peers and allows you to expand your personal success while building greater success for your organization.

Executive brands build trust by using their authenticity—the unedited scope of their strengths, skills, passion, and values. And they know how to identify and leverage the brands of their staff.

When these leaders liberate the individuality of each team member and then paint a picture of what can be achieved together, they infuse energy and excitement into every employee. They enthusiastically guide each person on the team to maximize individual performance and support mutual goals. Cindy Key, Senior Professional in Human Resources, and co-founder of career services firm Key Concepts, calls this "the power of unlocking uniqueness." We like the way Cindy describes what that means: "Unlocking the uniqueness hidden under the surface allows the team to accelerate success. They flourish, create amazing results, and—imagine this—they have fun!"

Even if you have no direct reports, there are opportunities to demonstrate leadership skills at all levels of the organization.

You likely know a team member who acts as the orchestra conductor, creating harmony in even the most discordant team. Or someone who has no direct reports yet skillfully brings a complicated project in on time and under budget. These people are authentic de facto leaders.

Eleanor was an individual contributor in product management who truly was a de facto leader. No one, including the team leader, would make a major move without running it by her. Her internal brand as "oracle" was so strong that her reputation was literally embedded in company lore.

Eleanor was intelligent and politically savvy—and she was a loyal team player, dedicated to the success of every member. When people on the team got stuck, they'd go to her; she always knew the right next step and could cut through any confusion with exactly the right solution. Team leaders would change, but each would eventually admit, "I'm technically the manager, but Eleanor runs the show."

Your executive brand is the key to enlightened leadership that inspires *and* produces.

Is YOUR leadership branded?

DARE | Be a leader, no matter your role. Fearlessly use who you are and what makes you unique to inspire the people around you and to impact your organization.

Peers Are Powerful:
Brand Within

Get out from behind the desk.

Gone are the days when you only had to please your manager and the CEO. Today, success means demonstrating your value to peers and colleagues throughout the *entire* organization. And it means leading outside your standard domain. It means becoming a role model for the people in finance even though you are the head of R&D.

Because organizations are getting comfortable with being virtual, it's easy to get lazy—but instant messaging was not designed for communicating with your colleague in the office or the cube next door. The best technology in the world cannot fully replace the value of face-to-face connections.

Here's some added incentive to go full-out for face-to-face. Getting up from behind the desk to meet with a colleague down the hall or on another floor is good for your internal brand equity *and*, more importantly, for your longevity. With recent research suggesting that sitting for more than three hours a day can shorten your life expectancy by two years, it seems that visiting a colleague, rather than picking up the phone or sending an email, is not only good branding, it's preventive medicine!

Even if face-to-face connections are not an option—and often they are not—regular connection with your colleagues is powerful. It helps you prove your worth, not only to your manager and team, but to your colleagues as well.

Jack Robbins, an IT executive who works remotely, says, "Today, there's a tendency to lean on email and instant messaging. Both are valuable tools and can help increase productivity, but I think it's important that you don't let them rule your day, your schedule, and your output. In my experience, many issues can be resolved much more quickly with a phone call than with a repetitive string of emails or ongoing instant messages. I try, as often as possible, to use email as a follow-up to my communications, rather than an introduction to them. While it may be an unintended benefit, voice communications build much stronger relationships among colleagues."

According to Roy Young, president of Beyond B-School and author of *Marketing Champions*, "Marketers must recognize that it's the equity that marketing builds *within* the organization, rather than the equity that marketing builds with customers, that often makes the difference between gaining a seat at the strategy table, on the one hand, and powerlessness and marginality on the other."

What's YOUR internal brand equity?

DITCH | Stop going it alone. Start connecting with your peers. They are your brand's internal PR machine. Give them something to shout about.

Leave the Office:

Be Seen

Out of sight really does mean out of mind.

Be fearless with face time! Visibility—internal and external—is critical to your brand and to your career momentum.

Increase your external visibility with your customers, your business partners, your peers in other companies, and *your* business community. Get to know these associates at all levels. Take active roles in professional organizations. Express your brand and maximize your strengths through leadership, speaking, writing, designing programs, blogging, and so on.

Face time—personal connection—is vanishing with the explosion of virtual communication tools. Step away from the virtual and into the real whenever possible. Personal connections are powerful and memorable, and there is no substitute for the reality of a warm handshake. When you must be virtual, seek ways to emulate personal connection. Today's sophisticated video and teleconferencing tools allow you to easily connect both visually and vocally to internal and external stakeholders.

When connecting, think *quality* over *quantity*. It is much more effective to belong to fewer organizations and take an active role in them than to spread your time among many organizations and remain on the sidelines. Taking on a board position or other visible role will enable you to form stronger connections with the membership.

One of Deb's executive clients, whom we'll call Cindy, experienced an unexpected relocation from California back to the Midwest to care for an ill parent—a multiple challenge of family move, eldercare, and job search. To jumpstart her network, Cindy immediately joined a local business group, arrived early at the first meeting to get acclimated, and jumped in to help one of the board members set up the room. After working together a bit and hearing her story, the board member asked Cindy if she'd consider taking on the program development role, which had been vacant for months for lack of a volunteer. Cindy jumped at the chance, knowing that planning programs and seeking speakers would give her immediate introductions (and access) to the area's business community. That instant network and visibility were instrumental in her landing a new job in record time.

If there is not a professional organization that appeals to you, start one. Being the founder of an organization is hard work, but it goes a long way toward building visibility, credibility, and network connections.

Increasing your external visibility builds your brand with the people who can impact your career now and in the future. It's all about career management.

Are you spending enough time out of the office?

DO | Every week, take time to meet face-to-face with a client, an external colleague, or a professional contact. Strong brands don't go into hiding; they know face time will help them flourish.

My Sparks

Record your ideas, sparked from Chapter 9.

Chapter Ten | What's Your Message?

SHOW

Be One of a Kind

Make Them Care

Say Hello to 3D STARS

Give 'Em a Reason to Invest:

Be One of a Kind

Not everyone wants you!

Reality check: In the world of work, no one cares about your personal brand until they know WHY they should care. In a market or organization flooded with top talent, why are YOU the best person to deliver it? Your job is to MAKE the right people care... to PROVE your skills and their value to the market, your employer, and your teams.

But how do you communicate that? How do you demonstrate your personal brand's unique promise of value in a way that demonstrates the *reality* of the promise? How do you combine your personal brand (who you are) *and* your business value (what you do and what happens when you do it)?

Enter the Why-Buy-ROI™, a simple but powerful way to communicate your unique branded value, created by Deb and leading career expert, Susan Whitcomb. Your Why-Buy-ROI (WBR for short) says, "Here's who I am. I know what you need right now, I've done it, here's how I did it, here's what happened when I did it, and I can do it again!"

Your Why-Buy-ROI makes you one of a kind . . . unique . . . because, like DNA, no one will have your exact combination of brand, value, and relevance. The *Why-Buy* is your brand—the "why-buy" YOU, when others can also deliver similar value. It builds chemistry and fit by telling employers and stakeholders who you are and how you make value happen. The *ROI* is the "make me care." It shows that when an employer invests in you, you will generate a steady return on that investment.

William's Why-Buy-ROI is "Passionate pioneer in human branding, enthusiastically empowering people to trust their individuality, communicate their unique value, and soar."

Now let's deconstruct it using the Why-Buy-ROI formula:

- **Here's who I am**—William is "a passionate pioneer in human branding."
- **I know what you need right now**—This is implied rather than stated. William knows that the people he attracts are looking for the ability to be successful and follow their dreams while being authentically themselves.
- **I've done it, here's how I did it**—William "enthusiastically empowers people to trust their individuality and communicate their unique value."
- **Here's what happened when I did it**—William's clients "soar!"
- **And I can do it again**—William's words hold such conviction and authenticity that there is no question he can do it again.

William's WBR is authentic; heartfelt; and delivers an emotional, believable connection that taps into people's deep need for significance and joy. And just the simple word "soar" slams the message home. The people and companies attracted by his WBR trust that he's a good investment.

Can you prove YOU are a good investment?

DARE | Celebrate your differences! Create your Why-Buy-ROI. What's unique and special about who you are and what you do? What does an employer get when he gets you? How are you valuable?

The Burden of Proof Is on YOU:

Make Them Care

Today's market mantra: Why you? So what? Make me care! And do it fast!

Make employers and leaders care by infusing your Why-Buy-ROI with the 3Bs of value—bold, brief, and branded!

State your wins **boldly**. Tell why they matter to your target audience. What do they get that they want and/or need? Demonstrate that in straightforward, simple terms that make it abundantly clear that you will be a good investment. For the humble, please know that it's not bragging if it's true—it's just fact. Simply say what happens, without grandiose pronouncements. Your actions will speak for themselves; trust that and let them speak.

Make your Why-Buy-ROI **brief** and specific. The more simply and concisely your actions are stated, the more loudly your actions speak.

Clearly **brand** your Why-Buy-ROI with valuable differentiation that supports the creation of your relevant value. You'll power the indefinable chemistry and fit that often make the hire.

Deb's Why-Buy-ROI is "Unabashedly passionate brand catalyst, propelling visionary, gutsy CEOs with a conscience to land faster, earn more, have fun, and change the world—without becoming sharks or suits!" (Twenty-seven bold, brief, and branded words.)

Let's deconstruct Deb's "So what? Make me care! Do it fast!" 3B Why-Buy-ROI:

- **Bold**—There's no ambiguity or false modesty when Deb says her clients "land faster, earn more, have fun, and change the world—without becoming sharks or suits!" Its simple, bold language is authentic to her and resonates with her targets.

- **Brief**—It's 27 words overall and just 10 words at its core—"passionate brand catalyst, propelling visionary, gutsy CEOs with a conscience."
- **Branded**—The brand attributes in Deb's WBR are very specific about who she is—an "unabashedly passionate brand catalyst"; who her clients are—"visionary, gutsy CEOs with a conscience"; and what her clients value—"land faster, earn more, have fun, and change the world—without becoming sharks or suits!"

If you believe who Deb is, if you're not a shark or a suit, and you've been seeking what she delivers, there's an almost chemical reaction of connection—a "Wow, I trust her, she gets me!" She has made you care and she has done it fast.

What's your "So what? Make me care! Do it fast!" 3B Why-Buy-ROI?

DITCH | Stop being long-winded and vague. Start speaking the bold, brief language of value. Bottom-line it! Your brand, company, and career will thank you for it.

Good-bye Flat:

Say Hello to 3D STARS

STARS stories tell, prove, and win.

According to psychologist Jerome Bruner, people are 20 times more likely to remember a fact if it is part of a story. Author Daniel Pink says, "Stories are easier to remember—because in many ways, stories are how we remember."

When relating *your* story, a STARS technique (Start, Tell, Anchor, Roundup, Slam) can make your accomplishments memorable. Here's an example, deconstructed:

- This year, we stopped the bleeding and saved the company's Midwest flagship store. *(START strong)*

- After two of the area's manufacturers closed, the store experienced six quarters of escalating losses. I was sent in to either save it or salvage it for sale. I went for "save it!" I knew three things: the store had been great; we had a top-notch, loyal sales force; and we needed to differentiate yet re-establish trust—fast—to attract the limited local dollars. *(TELL the challenges; start the plan)*

- We ran daily progress pep rallies, sought employee and customer suggestions, reworked the inventory, and instituted a loyalty program and a "You have the power!" customer service policy to give our sales force a "Nordstrom's" mentality and pride. We sponsored numerous local events to raise visibility for our community-focused "We're all in this together!" campaign and tied it to social media with specials and fun contests on Facebook and Twitter. *(ANCHOR your Why-Buy-ROI with actions)*

- Sales stabilized and morale increased by the end of Q1. By Q4, sales were up 20% (with healthy margins). Our loyalty program customers were increasing by 25% a quarter, and social media was attracting a new base of Millennials. *(ROUNDUP results)*

- We rescued the store, saved jobs, and were featured in a *Forbes* article, "Doing It Right in Small-City America," which our CEO credits for the company's DOW uptick. *(SLAM it home with strategic impact)*

Once written, a STARS like this can be edited into brief accomplishment statements for a performance review or resume, transformed into bio or social media profile content, or practiced as interview answers or networking conversations.

STARS storytelling compels action! Leaders, teams, and customers imagine you in a similar situation (theirs), achieving similar outcomes (for them). Your STARS get you closer to "sold!"

Can you "tell it to sell it?"

DO | Think about a time when you were in the zone, working your passion, making good things happen. Make your case using the STARS format to define the experience and value. Shine on!

My Sparks

Record your ideas, sparked from Chapter 10.

Chapter Eleven

SHOW

How Do You Say It?

Make an Exciting Entrance

Keep a Job Journal

Align Your STARS

Don't Bore 'Em with Job Titles:

Make an Exciting Entrance

Your introduction (or elevator pitch) is the opening line to your incredible story.

In the world of work, we introduce ourselves frequently—in meetings, with new clients or colleagues, and at professional association gatherings. But how many people do we bore? How many of them want to know more?

If someone introduced herself to you at a networking meeting by saying, "Hi, I'm a biologist and senior director of Bio Research at XYZ Pharmaceuticals," would that be enough to grab your attention? When you introduce yourself as your job title, you are a commodity—there are thousands of others (maybe even hundreds of thousands) who share that title, and you disappear among them.

Strong brands know who they are, the value they create, and what type of individuals and companies will likely find that value important. They introduce themselves to others, not by title, but by communicating what they deliver or the passion they have for what they do—and they modify it so it's relevant to each person they meet. They get noticed because their listeners become interested, intrigued, and want to know more.

What if our senior director of Bio Research said, "I manage a team of scientists who design drugs for very rare diseases and make a difference in people's lives. It's a great reason to go to work every day!" It's likely you'd be interested and want to know more.

And what if she were even more bold and exciting in her language? What if she said, with relish, "I battle bugs every day—the kind of bugs that cause rare diseases that make people really sick. My team and I won't rest until we've squashed them!" She hasn't mentioned her job title or company, but in 28 words, you already know a lot about her brand—you know that she's passionate, dedicated, smart, interesting, and a bit irreverent. And you want to know more. Who wouldn't?

Craft an intriguing introduction or elevator pitch using the 3Bs:

- **Bold**—Jolt and captivate them; get them hungry for more!
- **Brief**—Keep them awake; say it in no more than 30 words.
- **Branded**—Be YOU; include your unique brand.

Is your introduction a real snooze or a jolt of caffeine?

DITCH | Dump bland! Write a caffeinated, bold, brief, and branded introduction; practice it; and use it at your next meeting. Pay attention to the responses and revise if necessary. JOLT 'em!

Power Your Performance Review:

Keep a Job Journal

Most executives dread annual reviews.

Crafting a thorough and accurate performance review or 360 for your reports or peers is an ethical responsibility *and* a time drain in an all-too-short day.

Contributing to your own review is just as taxing.

Change the paradigm, win enduring gratitude from your boss and your team, and move your career forward! Make it easy for them (and your company) to remember, appreciate, and compensate your brilliance.

How? Keep a STARS job journal of your projects, challenges, and wins.

If you've read Chapter 10, Snap 3, you know that STARS stands for <u>S</u>tart strong, <u>T</u>ell the challenge, <u>A</u>nchor your brand, <u>R</u>oundup the results, and <u>S</u>lam home the impact. Using the STARS technique, you can journal your progress throughout the year and note the particulars of your challenges and wins—you can even do it for your reports or team.

Keeping a job journal doesn't have to be an arduous task—a few tickler words will often suffice. You can write out full STARS narratives in your job journal, or you can use your own variety of note taking. Consistency is the key—so determine a schedule for journaling, and keep it. Make entries weekly, monthly, or quarterly, but make them! You might even consider making job journaling a part of your nine-minutes-a-day plan.

Just be sure whatever method you use captures the challenge you faced, the actions you took, the immediate and strategic results you generated, and the way your brand connects to it all. Then when you craft the narrative or write the review, you'll remember the guts and the glory you need for the story.

Try to remember the details of what your individual reports have accomplished over a year. Not so easy, right? You've likely forgotten some critical pieces. If they're prepared, they'll remind you—or maybe they don't remember either. Do you want to be that forgettable, too?

Your job journal of STARS stories will help you easily assemble a brief and powerful recap of your (and your team's) growth and impact over the past year. You'll be able to give your team well-deserved recognition. You will make it easy for your boss (or the board, or your peers) to accurately complete your performance appraisal or 360 review, recommend promotion, and solidify new goals. When you negotiate compensation, you will do so from a true position of strength built on clear value.

Is your performance a dim memory or a bright star?

DITCH | Stop waiting until your annual review to define your contributions. Regularly document your projects, challenges, and victories—and track ROI! Be unforgettable!

Ace the Interview:

Align Your STARS

Every productive meeting relies on good communication—and an interview is just a meeting.

We've all been through boring, rambling meetings. We can't wait for them to be over, we're sorely tempted to multitask, and we resent the time we've been forced to waste.

Imagine you are in an interview. You are relaxed and prepared, chatting easily, yet you sense that the interviewer, who holds the key to your promotion or next position, seems a little disinterested and distracted. What you thought was going well begins to slide downhill. Now imagine you just lost the opportunity because you were not communicating your value in the way the interviewer needed to hear it. Ouch!

You don't want to be that person, but what can you do? How can you capture, and keep, the attention of any listener? You can lean in.

Here's how leaning in works: Consider a newspaper or Internet story—a compelling headline captures interest and leads into the body copy, and the body copy often has subheadings. Some of us read the headline; skim the subheads; and decide if we're interested enough to read further, come back to it later, or just leave it. Others absorb every detail. Still others fall somewhere in between.

The same is true in an interview, or even a client meeting (which is really an interview, right?). Some interviewers prefer the classic executive "bottom-line-it-for-me" style. Others want to skim the surface before taking a dive. Still others want it all and are prepared for a marathon conversation.

During the interview or meeting, you can use your STARS stories (remember Start, Tell, Anchor, Roundup, and Slam from Chapter 10?) to lean in and keep the attention of any listener, with any communication style.

Harness your desire to tell all! *Lean in* and use your STARS prep to capture attention by quickly headlining the result or strategic impact. Follow up with a *brief* overview of the challenge and your success strategies.

Then *lean back*, shut up, and wait. If your listener wants more, she'll ask for more. If she doesn't, you've given her what she needs. You won't have tried her patience or wasted her time.

Learn to lean in. You'll impress the bottom-line-it-for-me folks with your clarity and brevity. You'll push the "skim, then dive" folks into more questions, and you'll settle the "I want it all" folks into their chairs, ready to dig deep.

Do you have the courage to lean in, shut up, and wait?

DARE | Do the work that others don't or won't. Review your job journal; prepare your STARS stories; align them with what the interviewer needs to know. Practice your "lean in" delivery. Way to go, Ace!

My Sparks

Record your ideas, sparked from Chapter 11.

Chapter Twelve

How Do You Document It?

SHOW

Brand Your Resume

Brand Your Bio

Put Your Best Face Forward

Defy Mediocrity:
Brand Your Resume

The traditional resume is a dead retread.

Most people don't know that the traditional resume is belly-up. You're smarter than that! You know that the resume never was a magic bullet and now it's not even a first-strike document. In the age of LinkedIn, Google, and social media, by the time the reader sees your resume, it's often a bland, late-to-the-game confirmation of previous impressions—a retread of what is already known.

Yet a resume, no matter how diminished in importance, is still likely to be the single most requested career document in your executive tool kit—and we're not just talking about transitions. Your resume is valuable inside your company—for moving internally, configuring teams, and building your brand. So beat out bland and go for bold. Make your resume speak for you—with your brand and ROI—with speed. Why speed? As noted career expert and bestselling author Susan Whitcomb observes, "Social media and the bombardment of info-overload have caused many people to have the attention span of a lit match." In other words, say it quick to make it stick!

When crafting your resume for this new world of "So what? Make me care! Do it fast!" you need to know your brand, your ROI value, and the employer's wants, upfront, *before* you write; only then can you craft your marketing message (your pitch) and form your content strategy. Focus on impact and the accomplishments that created it. Keep the essentials, nothing else. Tell what needs to be told. Boldly dump the rest.

Here are 10 tips for crafting a "So what? Make me care! Do it fast!" resume for internal stakeholders or external markets.

1. Accept that your resume is not a history or biography; it's marketing. Have a strategy for your market.
2. Marketing strategy means knowing your targets' needs, how your Why-Buy-ROI fits, and whether you need multiple resumes.
3. We know you are brilliant, but you can't include it all! Your strategy must guide your content decisions.
4. Think of potential content as helpful, valuable, or critical. Showcase "critical," edit down "valuable," and dump "helpful."
5. "Critical" usually means delivering ROI or supporting the delivery of ROI. Research will tell you which ROI matters.
6. Replace the objective with a profile; objectives waste space.
7. A good profile is a magnetic "career brief" with a career snapshot, a Why-Buy-ROI, and an accomplishment or two.
8. Replace "responsible for" job descriptions with "stats snaps"—quick views of P&L, reports, divisions managed, etc.
9. Ruthlessly edit, set aside, then edit again. Think: can it be shorter, more powerful, more branded? Don't rush this step!
10. Think IMPACT—highlight the ONE best thing you did in each job (critical); support it with accomplishments (valuable).

Ruthlessly editing your resume to reach the nirvana of bold, branded brevity is a *tough* job, but you can do it! Bonus? Your resume will be easily readable on a tablet or smartphone (which more than 90% of CEOs carry). And don't you want to be in the CEO's pocket?

Do you have the courage to stand out and surprise? To tell only what needs to be told?

DARE | Be willing to slash and trash! Pretend your value message has to fit on a business card. Edit, edit, edit, and see what happens! Chances are that bold and brief will get belief!

Catalyze Chemistry:

Brand Your Bio

Your bio should be the voice of your brand when you're not there.

In a world of stilted and bland "corporate speak," the most effective career marketing document for today's executive is fast becoming the *branded bio*—a personal marketing tool with a strong Why-Buy-ROI—that not only demonstrates tangible accomplishments but also builds intangible chemistry.

Where a resume and traditional bio focus nearly 100% on experience, contributions, and credentials (often with a boring string of accomplishments), an effective *branded* bio truly reflects you—a unique, 3D, whole person. By focusing some attention on the passions and interests that define you, it expresses your value *and* your personality.

If you're used to a traditional bio, you may relate to John, an executive who participated in one of Reach's personal branding talent development programs. A colleague asked John to send his bio to a potential client, but his most up-to-date version was the branded bio he'd just completed. He was concerned that it might be perceived as "really out there" but sent it to the client, who responded, "Interesting bio—even just the way it is written." He suggested a meeting, and John won the business.

Think about what attracts us in life—people and things that are interesting, unusual, unique, passionate, brilliant, and beautiful. Don't hide what makes you special because of a misplaced idea of what defines "professional." The most compelling and effective branded bios create connection through their authentic humanity. So get brave and be YOU!

Consider the branded bio of Deb's client "Eureka Jack" Neigel—innovator, inventor, and transformation agent (you'll meet him again in Chapter 13). Jack's bio begins with this engaging entry: "It all started with worms." The bio then covers the highlights of Jack's vastly varied career (and early years growing up on a ranch) and ends with: "Always independent, and as comfortable in the boardroom as he is on the back of a quarter horse herding cattle (or influencing night crawlers), this 6'2" former linebacker is well known for wearing a variety of exotic-skin cowboy boots. He jokes that he uses them to 'Kick the hell out of the status quo!' And, of course, he researches and invents for fun. He just can't help it." We *dare you* to *not* want to know more about Jack!

Like Jack, you can (and should) be the professional *and* personal you in your bio (yes, even in the annual report). Combine *who you are, what you do,* and *the value you create when you do it,* with *the passions you hold, the things you enjoy,* and *the background that helped shape you*. And write in your voice. You may be tempted to default to your usual language—corporate speak—but don't give in; beat the corporate out of your bio! It may take some time to de-program, but, with determination, it will happen.

When your bio gets personal—when you boldly move from bland to branded—you are differentiated, human, and interesting. You build connection, trust, and relevance. You are valued. You catalyze chemistry. You soar.

Is your bio bland or branded? Soaring or boring?

DARE | Get uncomfortable. Get out of the box. Rewrite your bio, drop corporate speak, and brand it in your voice. You'll attract the *right* people to the *real* you.

Strong Brands Are Recognizable:
Put Your Best Face Forward

It's great to connect a face with a name.

The Internet and technology have enabled virtual global workplaces, yet it is now more difficult to *visually* connect with coworkers and stakeholders. Unlike the halls of traditional organizations or the geographically contained villages of the past where you would recognize everyone, these new paradigms are made up of many faceless inhabitants.

Strong brands are visually recognizable. Give your virtual connections an opportunity to see who you are with a high-quality headshot, which not only shows your face, but also says a lot about your brand through your use of color, background, clothing and hairstyle, textures, and other visual clues.

When we say high quality, we mean a professionally taken photo that reflects you in a positive and professional light yet exudes a sense of personality, a sense of who you are. Just don't get too personal. We're not talking about the snapshot your mother took of you at your last family beach outing.

Your headshot can appear in many places. In addition to accompanying your branded bio or appearing in the annual report or other corporate materials, your headshot is a critical component of every online profile you build, making you more real and more recognizable in a world that is fast becoming more virtual. Nearly every site where you create an online account—including Facebook, Twitter, LinkedIn, and your company intranet—requires you to upload a photo. If you don't, people wonder why you didn't and may even assume you have something to hide.

Laura Smith-Proulx, award-winning writer, author, national columnist, and LinkedIn enthusiast, surveyed recruiters who actively source candidates on LinkedIn. She writes: "I found that the subject of profiles that are 'missing' a photo stirs some intense feelings." Here's a typical response to Laura's survey: "Personally, I don't give much credence to those profiles that do not have a photo," stated Will Armstrong of Serco, Inc. "I have to wonder what they are trying to hide, and I feel less connected to them."

Headshots aren't just for social media—your company wants you to have a professional headshot. In fact, when William develops corporate personal branding programs, he's often asked to bring a photographer for participants' headshots.

When planning your professional headshot, think outside of the light box! Don't play it safe: If your colleagues' photos are shot in the boardroom, ask the photographer to take yours on the factory floor, in the shop that sells your product, or at another relevant location. If your profession is nontraditional, think about a shot that shows you engaged in an on-brand sport or activity like sailing, playing an instrument, or constructing a home for Habitat for Humanity. Either way, your headshot will say: memorable, engaging, on brand!

What does your headshot say about *you*?

DO | Be authentic, but save the candids for your private Facebook page. Get a professionally taken photograph that reinforces your brand. Seeing your face inspires confidence and trust.

My Sparks

Record your ideas, sparked from Chapter 12.

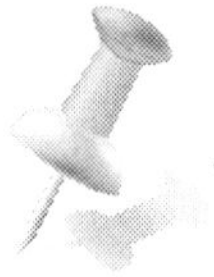

Chapter Thirteen

How Do You Package Your Message?

SHOW

Vocalize Your Identity

Have a Signature Color

Have a Trademark You™

Visuals Speak Volumes:
Vocalize Your Identity

Your brand identity system is the visual vocabulary of your brand.

Your employer understands the importance of developing and consistently applying its brand identity system. You see the company logo, colors, fonts, and other imagery every day—and you instantly recognize them. When you're communicating on behalf of your organization, you need to use your company's brand identity system. But for *your* non-work-related communications, you need your own visual vernacular: your *personal* brand identity—the packaging that conveys your brand message—the wrapper that reinforces your brand.

Communicating your personal brand requires a visual brand identity system that encompasses each of the ways in which you represent yourself to others. Your visual identity system reinforces and augments the content of your message. When you consistently use visual identity aids like brand-appropriate colors, fonts, and images in all your communications, you make it easier for people to recognize you. Identify the elements that best express your personal brand, and then consistently customize your online profiles (blog, website, Twitter background, YouTube channel, etc.) and traditional career marketing tools with your brand identity to ensure brand recognition.

Deb's client "Eureka Jack" Neigel, whom you met in Chapter 12, needed a brand identity system that would visualize his wide-ranging background and huge personality. Jack thinks of cool new ways to create things, do things, and solve things. He's an inventor and innovator who has developed some of the world's most useful innovations (many of which are so classified he can't tell Deb what they are). He's an ex-Marine, a nuclear energy pro, a tough-turnarounds specialist, a transformative thinker, and an advisor to leaders around the globe. He grew up on a quarter horse ranch in Minnesota. He wears exotic-skin cowboy boots (often red) nearly every day. His laugh is as big as all outdoors and his energy is contagious. He's a billion-dollar innovation flywheel. But what does that *look* like?

Jack is *not* a black and white guy. He couldn't fade into the woodwork if he tried. He and Deb worked on colors, fonts, and formats that would reflect his extreme differentiation. They discovered that for Jack, orange and red best expressed his massive creativity, energy, and determination.

His new visual identity system is cohesive and conveys the *real* Jack. His letterhead and consulting company brochure are saturated with red and orange touches. His bio and all other career documents are headed with orange and red bands of color with his name (presented as a graphical "Eureka Jack" personal logo) and his tagline. His resume headings are red or orange color blocks that replace conventional headings with "Who, Why, What, When, How." His typeface is Gill Sans, a modern font. His signature personal item is that pair of red cowboy boots; they appear in photographs in his brochures. Jack's brand identity system reflects and enhances who he is, how he acts, what he does, and how he makes people feel. The congruity is unmistakable and memorable—like Jack.

What do you need to put in place to be visually memorable—to develop a strong and consistent visual identity?

DO | Power your brand! Invest time and effort in developing a strong visual identity system. Consistently apply it to all your communications. Use it until it feels like your own skin.

Color Evokes Emotion:

Have a Signature Color

Color is powerful.

Every successful company understands the strong influence of color. Think "Big Blue" or "What can Brown do for you?" Color is just as important for personal branding. Vincent Van Gogh wrote, "I have, just like everyone else, a feeling for the power of color."

Your signature color expresses your brand attributes, evokes emotion, and builds that all-important connection with the people who surround your brand. It's such an important part of your brand identity system that we single it out here.

Through strategic application of your signature color, your business cards, stationery, thank-you notes, resume, executive portfolio, email signature, and website—even your office décor and clothing—become a cohesive suite of personal marketing tools.

William worked with an ad agency's creative director whose expertise and brand differentiation were focused on color. She was a genius at putting together color palettes for brochures and websites, and color was such a major part of her brand that even her clothes communicated her expertise. She always wore outfits that included a color and its complement—she would pair a red dress with a green scarf, or enhance a blue pantsuit with orange accessories. These color choices were probably lost on most people, but her ability to use color to make a statement was abundantly clear to her target audience of designers.

To make the most of your color, ensure that the color you choose is

- **Accurate**—Choose a color because it best expresses your brand attributes, not because it's your favorite.

- **Relevant**—Ensure your brand color is significant and compelling to your target audience.
- **Culturally Correct**—Make sure your color works in all parts of the world where you plan to work or do business.
- **Applied Consistently**—Always use the same shade and hue. And know the PMS, RGB, and CMYK formulas.

As you read in the previous snap, Jack Neigel takes branding with color a step further, fusing *two brand colors*—his signature red and orange—*into one brand color impression*. He never uses one without the other—all of his documents, brochures, business cards, and web presence contain both. Three of his attributes—energy, potency, and determination—are both red *and* orange attributes, and his other "red" attributes of action, passion, courage, power, desire, and love align with additional "orange" attributes of productivity, force, strength, vitality, success, and encouragement. The similarities are so congruent that Jack can use both colors as one.

What's *your* signature brand color?

DO

Discover your signature brand color (watch www.bit.ly/brand color); then use it! Branding all your visual communications with your signature color evokes a strong emotional brand response. Color your world!

Be Memorable:

Have a Trademark You™

Trademarks communicate your brand attributes, creating congruence between your message and your packaging.

Often, you are identified by those items that have just become part of who you are, what you say, and how you behave. We all know Martha Stewart's "It's a good thing," the Intel four-note signature sound, and Paris Hilton's chihuahua. As for logos, we know "O" is for Oprah.

A trademark can be an image, graphic, texture, catchphrase, sound, accessory, or even your name stylized as a logo. Images and graphics help you communicate complex ideas simply. Textures are great for backgrounds.

Jennifer Bayon is a sales executive for the cosmetics company Yes to Carrots. One of Jennifer's most prominent and visible brand attributes is her curiosity—she is an interesting and *interested* collector of new ideas. Anyone who has spent time with Jennifer—whether in a meeting or out to dinner—has seen her writing in her trademark notebook, jotting down ideas, reminders, and things she wants to learn more about, synthesize, and turn into action.

You probably know someone at your company like Jennifer—someone who has a recognizable trademark. William worked with an ad exec who always wore red socks. One of our colleagues wears vintage jewelry every day. William is always recognizable in a sleek dark suit and crisp open-collared shirt (he never wears a tie). One of Deb's CEO clients ends every email with a daily inspirational quote, signed in his signature color. Deb is known for a love of bright clothing (especially her signature orange) and uniquely designed faux pearl jewelry. And you've met her client Jack Neigel—memorable for his "Eureka Jack" moniker and his red exotic-skinned cowboy boots.

To be as memorable, follow these steps:

1. If you don't have a trademark, or if your existing trademark leaves something to be desired, develop one that is congruent with who you are and what you want to be known for.

2. Apply it consistently in both real and virtual world communications—in meetings, PowerPoint presentations, or online social networking profiles; on your website or blog; through your clothing, accessories, or office design—wherever it makes sense.

3. Use your trademark repetitively for brand recognition. You may tire of it, but chances are your audience has barely experienced it.

Are you bold enough to create and parade your trademark?

DITCH | Stop thinking trademarks are for companies and celebrities. Walk on the wild side—create an authentic, brand-appropriate trademark and flaunt it! Get people to recognize brand *you*.

My Sparks

Record your ideas, sparked from Chapter 13.

Chapter Fourteen

How Do You Package Your World?

SHOW

Make It Shout

Brand Your Office

Brand Your Environment

Appearance Counts:
Make It Shout

Clothes DO make the man or woman!

Who we are is more important than how we look—of course, that is true. Yet when people meet us for the first time, they make an *instant* judgment.

First impressions last. In fact, it takes up to 20 more interactions with you to change the opinion formed in a first meeting. You need to be conscious of your appearance at all times.

One of William's clients, who works at a "very casual" high-tech giant, traded in his corporate uniform of flip flops, t-shirt, and shorts for khakis, loafers, and a button-down shirt. He found that his colleagues started treating him differently—with more respect!

Appearance is an important brand tool. Shift your focus to brand-specific apparel and accessories—clothes, non-verbal gestures, and movements are powerful brand statements.

One of the Reach-certified Personal Branding Master Strategists, Valerie Sokolosky, summed it up with this story: "A client, Mary, had great technical skills but lacked the 'polish' needed to be considered for advancement. We identified the core brand messages she wanted to leave in the hearts and minds of others and strategized ways she could update her appearance to show those attributes.

New clothing, hair, and makeup stayed true to Mary's brand, but boosted her confidence and showed her as a poised woman on the move. Within seven years, Mary progressed from a mid-level manager to the president of one of the company's divisions. Lesson learned? Paying attention to how you dress is important in projecting a strong personal brand, reflecting confidence and self-care, and leading others to take you more seriously."

If we ignore appearance, we risk confusing others about our brand; if we use appearance wisely, we help people better understand who we are—without saying a word.

Does your appearance communicate a confident, clear, on-brand message?

DITCH | Ruthlessly edit your wardrobe. Keep only the pieces that work; then add on-brand clothes and accessories that feel comfortable, give you confidence, work with your brand color, and are appropriate for your target audience. You'll quietly shout!

Your Surroundings Speak:

Brand Your Office

Does your office express what makes you unique, or are you out-of-place in your own space?

When you walk into someone's office, do you make judgments about them from what you see on their walls or desk? Most of us do. In fact, people are remarkably accurate at guessing others' personalities just by looking at their desks.

Take a good look at your office. What does it say about you? Don't be afraid to personalize your surroundings. Give yourself permission (and set aside the necessary time) to transform your desk and office (or cube) into truly brand-defining spaces.

If your brand is global and you have overseas responsibilities or aspirations to lead an overseas team, be sure your office reflects your brand with travel-related items like photos, a world-time clock, and work-appropriate memorabilia from trips. If you want to be seen as a candidate for the C-suite, de-clutter and dress your office for the part with upscale desk accessories and décor.

Maria, a business development executive at a major retailer, had a goal—to lead the company's international operations. She also had a problem. Being seen as global was critical to achieving her goal, yet though she spoke several languages and traveled the world, no one knew it. She decided to use her office to demonstrate how international she was. She had her Italian newspaper, the *Corriere Della Sera*, delivered at work instead of at home. She hung up four clocks; labeled them Hong Kong, Paris, New York, and San Francisco; and set them to the appropriate times. She sifted through her travel photos, selected those that showed her at various iconic places—like the Petronas Towers in Kuala Lumpur, the Arc de

Triomphe in Paris, and Corcovado in Rio de Janeiro—and placed them on her walls. It wasn't long before people started seeing her as truly global.

If your company has strict policies about what you can or cannot do in your office, don't despair. There is always a way to express your brand through your surroundings. If you can't paint your walls red, decorate your cubicle, or make your desk round, get creative. Use a special screen saver, rotate the one photo you're allowed to have, showcase the books you are reading, or even have a coffee mug or water bottle personalized with a brand color or quote.

The more clearly your office reflects your brand, the more firmly your brand is cemented in the minds of those who visit your workspace.

Are your personal style and office environment congruent with your brand?

DARE | Live in the inquiry; constantly assess. Are your surroundings on- or off-brand? Be bold! Commit to making your office, cubicle, or workspace energize you and beef up your brand.

Think Beyond the Office:
Brand Your Environment

Everything you touch or choose says something about your brand.

The special pen you use, the restaurant where you host client meetings, the hotels you choose for business travel—each of these things is revealing.

Companies know this and carefully select brand associations to bolster or augment their brand attributes. McDonald's coffee is Newman's Own; American Airlines' sandwiches are from Boston Market; BMW's car stereos are high-end Harman Kardon audio systems; the Ritz-Carlton uses Bulgari toiletries in their club-floor rooms. Starbucks' tea is Tazo—in fact, Tazo became so associated with Starbucks' brand that Starbucks bought the company!

When brand attributes are similar or the same, each synergistically *reinforces the other's shared attribute*. For instance, both W Hotels and Bliss Spa share the brand attribute of "trendy." Featuring Bliss Spa products in all W Hotel bathrooms boosts W's brand attribute of "trendy" and confirms guests' belief in the brand.

When brands are different, an appropriate partnership *connects to an aspirational brand attribute* that is valuable to the target audience. For example, when Kohl's decided to partner with Vera Wang to produce an affordable high-fashion clothing line, they added "fashion-forward" to their foundational brand attributes—and attracted new customers.

When Jose, an industrial product manager in Miami, wanted to add "tech-savvy" to his list of differentiating attributes, he searched for places in the city where "techies" hung out—focusing on cafes with

WiFi and a visible tech buzz (not just from the coffee). When he stumbled upon one close to the office, he started holding meetings there—for his team, and with his internal clients—using his new iPad to present his ideas and spark discussion. This simple strategy not only helped others see him as the team's tech expert, but he started to see himself that way as well. Jose's ownership of his "tech-savvy" attribute gave him the courage to continue to advance his skills in technology areas that would help him do his job better and, in doing so, stand out from his colleagues.

When making decisions about everything in your brand environment, be clear about whether you're looking to reinforce your brand or, like Jose, connect it with aspirational attributes that are desirable to your target audience.

Reinforce? Connect? Aspire? What's your plan?

DO

Assess everything you use on a typical day—from the pen you carry, to the car you drive, to the places you host meetings. If they are off-brand, decide how you will change them. Strong brands know that even little things make a big difference!

My Sparks

Record your ideas, sparked from Chapter 14.

My SHOW

Go-time Grid

Learning has little value without action!

Go back to the ditch, dare, and do sparks that you documented after each chapter in SHOW. Break them into tasks you can put on your "do-list." Use the table below to describe the task, assign it a priority, and note the date by which you will complete it.

You can document your thoughts here, or download the PDF version of this chart at ditchdaredo.com/resources.

Ditch, Dare, or Do	Priority	Concrete action I will take	What do I want to achieve from it?	Date

Ditch, Dare, or Do	Priority	Concrete action I will take	What do I want to achieve from it?	Date

GROW

Don't Be the World's Best-Kept Secret

Grow Your Brand:

Don't Be the World's Best-Kept Secret

Now that you KNOW who you are and have a system to SHOW your value message to your brand community, it's time to GROW—to further demonstrate what makes you exceptional and expand the influence of your brand. That means building your real- and virtual-world communications plan so you can continue to build and bolster your brand.

Use what you've learned about yourself and your brand community in Parts One and Two to

Stay focused and **clear**.

Deliver your brand promise **consistently**.

Be **constantly** visible to your target audience.

These three Cs of branding—clarity, consistency, and constancy—will help you grow your brand.

Your growth will come in improved visibility, an expanded fan club, increased serendipity, and more on-brand opportunities. With deliberate and steady communications, your brand will take on a life of its own. People will start to know who you are, and sometimes you'll have no idea how they found you! This gives you choices, perspectives, and contacts you may not have known about but will be thrilled to have.

In Part Three, GROW, you'll learn to spur growth by creating your real-world communications plan, understanding your online reputation, building your brand on the web, and using video to be present even when you're not there. These tools will keep you constantly visible to your network and to those who are making decisions about you. You'll be positioned as the go-to expert for that around which you've built your brand.

As leaders like Nelson Mandela, Suze Orman, Bill Clinton, Tony Robbins, Barack Obama, Anderson Cooper, and others have done, you too will build success by steadfastly communicating your brand. Without their commitment to consistent brand communication, the strengths, convictions, ideas, and contributions of these leaders would have gained little trust or recognition. Join them!

QUICK QUIZ

Before you dig into GROW, rate how you are currently exuding your brand.

Rate how you are exuding your brand.				
Strongly Disagree				**Strongly Agree**
I publish or e-publish articles/blogs regularly.				
1	2	3	4	5
I am an attentive listener.				
1	2	3	4	5
I deliver presentations to my target audience regularly.				
1	2	3	4	5
I google myself regularly and know how I show up on the web.				
1	2	3	4	5
My social network profiles are up-to-date and reflect my brand.				
1	2	3	4	5
When appropriate, I use video as a communications tool.				
1	2	3	4	5
I have a strong professional network, and I regularly stay in touch with and help the members.				
1	2	3	4	5

Total: ______

OK, this one is tougher. You likely scored lower than in the previous chapters. Whatever your score, jump in. Take what you learned about yourself in KNOW and the focus and packaging you gained in SHOW and get ready to GROW your brand!

Chapter Fifteen

GROW

Create Your Real-World Communications

Publish or Perish

Speak Out!

Listen to Express Yourself

Be a Thought Leader:

Publish or Perish

Publishing is not just for professors.

If you think that doing a good job, leading your team internally, and focusing on your customers is enough, think again.

No matter your position, for your brand to grow, you must extend your reach. Be a leader within your domain! Express your brand beyond your traditional constituencies into a broader, yet targeted audience.

If you're a finance director, bolster your brand by building a reputation with other finance directors. If you're an individual contributor, you'll want to demonstrate your technical expertise and express your point of view.

If you are a CEO, your job requires personal and corporate visibility that reaches globally—far beyond the people with whom you can personally connect.

Consider the thought leadership of one of Deb's former clients, Raphael Louis Vitón, president and partner of Maddock Douglas, "The Agency of Innovation." Raphael and his Maddock Douglas partner, Mike Maddock, recently co-authored *Free the Idea Monkey—To Focus on What Matters Most* and are the long-time writing team behind *BusinessWeek.com*'s "Innovation Engine" column, as well as contributors to *Forbes.com*'s Entrepreneur section. Raphael also contributes to the Maddock Douglas "Innovation Engine" blog.

The content and consistency of Raphael's publications support his brand and cement his credibility—and in doing so, support the Maddock Douglas brand as well.

Publishing articles, white papers, and blogs cement your thought leadership by getting your brand in front of your peers, your customers, your boss, and your *next* boss.

It's useful to remember that old adage that says each of us has a book (or a blog) inside. Book publishing can be an involved process, but writing and publishing a book is an incredible differentiator that extends your brand, empowers your mission, energizes your career, and drives company momentum.

Take a tip from Raphael: "We're on a crusade to help inspired leaders use innovation to change the world. So to help them, we write articles to inspire and empower their curiosity. We believe that helping leaders create positive change is a great investment, so our writing and content distribution has become a priority for us."

The pen is mightier than the sword. When was the last time you put pen to paper (or fingers to keyboard)?

DO | Put your ideas in print. Regular publishing increases your credibility and visibility. It establishes your position as a thought leader. Set aside time each week to write; you'll be surprised by what you can accomplish.

Fear Not:
Speak Out!

In the list of fears, public speaking is ranked just before death.

Comedian Jerry Seinfeld jokes that when we're at a funeral, we would rather be in the coffin than delivering the eulogy. But public speaking is no joke; it is one of the most persuasive business skills. It's one of your best opportunities to express your brand. It enables you to emotionally connect with your audience in a way that is more valuable than any other.

In-person communication affords a unique opportunity to truly connect in a world that is becoming more and more virtual. Whether to audiences of 3 or 3,000, the power of in-person communication is second to none. Face-to-face communication potently expresses, engages, inspires, entertains, and informs. It doesn't hurt your visibility, either!

In personal branding, we often talk about maximizing your brand's strengths, mitigating only those weaknesses that can hurt your brand. However, a weakness in public speaking requires mitigation no matter what brand attributes or organizational role you hold—if you are a poor public communicator, you're hindering your chances for advancement.

One of William's clients—let's call her Maryann—was so afraid of public speaking that she avoided it like Superman avoided Kryptonite. Before meetings where she was scheduled to present, she would "get sick" and ask a colleague to fill in. She hid from any job that might involve it, but after turning down two promotions that required public speaking, she realized she was severely limiting her growth potential. She considered anti-anxiety medication or hypnosis. Ultimately, desperation gave her the courage to dive in and start speaking. Rather than beginning in her work environment, she decided it would be less stressful to take on short speeches for the children's organization she supported. She began with brief presentations to her peers and progressed to longer presentations to potential donors. Now, Maryann doesn't run from presentations at work and believes she'll actually enjoy them one day.

If public speaking isn't your strongest communication aptitude (or if, like Maryann, you're deathly afraid of it), practice, practice, practice. The humorist Kin Hubbard asked, "Why doesn't the fellow who says 'I'm no speechmaker' let it go at that instead of giving a demonstration?" If Kin was speaking about you, invest in training through Toastmasters, a media coach, or other professional organizations.

Ralph Waldo Emerson said, "The eloquent man is he who is no eloquent speaker, but who is inwardly drunk with a certain belief." Passion for the power of personal branding and a deep desire to share it helped Deb overcome decades of public-speaking anxiety. "In childhood, and for years beyond, I was afraid of my own shadow," she says, laughing. "Now I coach CEOs, conduct personal branding workshops, and deliver keynote presentations. I'm still amazed that I can do it—that I *want* to do it—and I love it!"

Passion can help you, too. Use it to overcome your fear of public speaking, get you out of the gate, and propel you to eloquence.

All charismatic leaders use in-person communications to engage and activate others. Do you?

DARE | Within the next month, take courage in hand. Volunteer to speak at your office or at a professional association. Even if your knees are shaking, only you will know. Here comes charisma!

Succeed by Being Quiet:
Listen to Express Yourself

Contrary to what some believe, personal branding is not all about broadcasting.

Receiving is just as important.

In the first century, the Greek philosopher Epictetus said, "We have two ears and one mouth so that we can listen twice as much as we speak." It's just as true today. Listening is part of effective communication and critical to good branding.

When you listen, your attention is a differentiating characteristic in a frenetic, multitasking world. When you listen, you show others that you care about what they're saying. When you listen, you create an emotional connection.

Listening—really listening—to your employees and peers shows them that you respect *their* opinions. Actively listening to your clients shows them that you have *their* best interests in mind. Listening also shows your understanding that delivering *your* brand message means first letting others be heard.

In his blog post, "Leadership and the Power of Listening," Mike Myatt, author of *Leadership Matters... The CEO Survival Manual*, says, "...it is simply not possible to be a great leader without being a great communicator. This partially accounts for why we don't encounter great leadership more often. The big miss for most leaders is they fail to understand the purpose of communication is not to message, but to engage—THIS REQUIRES LISTENING." Mike continues, "When you reach the point in your life where the lightbulb goes off, and you begin to understand knowledge is not gained by flapping your lips, but by removing your ear wax, you have taken the first step to becoming a skilled communicator."

The best way to demonstrate that you're listening is to first provide visual clues, like nodding or smiling, and to then repeat what you have heard. But don't interrupt! Let the speaker finish speaking and let yourself finish listening before you begin to speak.

Stephen Covey said, "Most people do not listen with the intent to understand. They listen with the intent to reply." Fight the urge to respond until you have heard all of what the speaker has to say. And ask questions. Asking is a part of listening. Asking shows the speaker you are engaged.

We'll leave you with this sage advice from Mike Myatt's post: "A key point for all leaders to consider is that it's impossible to stick your foot in your mouth when it's closed. Think about it . . . when was the last time you viewed a negative sound bite of a CEO who was engaged in active listening?"

As President Calvin Coolidge often remarked, "I have noticed that nothing I never said did me any harm."

Are *you* ready to listen? *Really* listen?

DO | Do less talking. Really. Do more listening. Active listening gets you heard (and it keeps your foot out of your mouth)!

My Sparks

Record your ideas, sparked from Chapter 15.

Chapter Sixteen

Understand Your Online Reputation

GROW

Be Digitally Distinct

Stand Out

Be You in 3D

Increase Your Online Presence and Relevance:

Be Digitally Distinct

It's okay to have an ego, especially online! In fact, it's imperative.

Ego-surfing is good Google hygiene—and for strong brands, it's a required Google habit. If you don't ego-surf, you can't manage your Google presence (to you skeptics out there, yes, you *can* manage your Google presence), and if you don't manage your Google presence, you're leaving your brand unattended, destined to flounder.

Managing your Google presence means *understanding* what people are looking for when they google you, *seeing* what they find in a current search, and then *controlling* what they will find in a future search (yes, we did say control!).

When someone googles you, although they may not realize it, they use two primary factors to make decisions about you: volume of content (how much) and relevance of content (how specific). Your job as self-appointed Google brand manager is to meet those two factors with powerful on-brand content.

Fred, a publishing executive, found out why volume and relevance are important. When Fred googled himself, he was shocked to see that the only items that showed up were related to his previous career in real estate. Talk about an issue with relevance—how could any client in the world of publishing take him seriously when the most common words his Google search revealed were "raised ranch," "foreclosure," and "open house"?

Fred launched a "relevance recovery effort" to replace the Former Fred with the Future Fred, over time, by augmenting that blast from the past with "presence from the present." He updated all his online profiles with his publishing industry position and background, taking care to include those he'd not visited in months or years. To build more volume and a visible brand in the publishing community, he began contributing his opinions and comments to popular publishing industry blogs, and even started his own blog.

When, like Fred, you need to build your brand or augment it with new information, seek the right mix of volume and relevance. **Volume** speaks to how much content about you there is on the web. The more there is, the more people believe you have something to say. If you need increased *volume*, set up social networking profiles on many sites by editing your current branded bio and establishing accounts at Visible.me, Ziki.com, and Ziggs.com, to name a few.

Quality trumps quantity, so **relevance** is even more important. Relevance refers to how consistently the search results align with who you say you are or with the person for whom the searcher is looking. To enhance *relevance*, do as Fred did—update your profiles, write, blog, comment on blogs, and even review books related to your area of expertise at high-traffic sites like Amazon.com and Barnesandnoble.com. You'll build up relevant, compelling content that serves your present profession and pushes down content that is unflattering or inconsistent.

Are you relevant? Is your *virtual* you in line with the *real* you?

DARE | Ego surf once a week—every week! Look at the first three pages of your results. Do they truly represent your brand? If not, take action. Fast.

Don't Get Lost in the Crowd: Stand Out

If your name is James Taylor and you're not the famous singer, you have some online branding work to do.

The web is a crowded place and it's becoming more crowded every day. According to worldwidewebsize.com, at the time this book was written, the indexed web contained nearly eight billion pages.

The huge rush of people getting their brands online has caused a great deal of brand confusion. Google results are rarely pure because virtually every professional has posted a profile, blog comment, or article. This creates complexity for those who want to learn about you and need to determine the content they should associate with you. Add to that the mix-ups spurred by sharing a common name or sharing a celebrity name—or worse, sharing a name with a notorious criminal—and without intervention, your brand might as well be mired in mud.

Fortunately, there's hope. Most web searchers are sophisticated enough to know when Google results reveal a jumble of people with your name. They will likely refine the search by adding a keyword or phrase they would associate with you.

That's exactly what Kelly Welch, an executive coach and Reach-certified Personal Branding Strategist, realized. Kelly shares her name with an acupuncturist, a doctor, and, um …an adult entertainer. It makes it hard for those who are trying to find her to be able to contact her. And even worse, it confuses those who may not be patient enough to find the right Kelly Welch or to identify which content they should associate with her.

So, Kelly decided to make sure everything she posts on the web has the phrase "personal branding" in it. Now, google "Kelly Welch personal branding" and you'll find more than 95% of the entries on the first five pages are about her!

The more crowded the web and the more common your name, the more important it is to include keywords or phrases related to your area of expertise in everything you post. Without them, you might be anyone. With them, you're *you*.

What's *your* keyword or phrase?

DO | Help the real you be found. Identify your keywords and include them in everything you post. And don't get complacent; be sure to review and refine them regularly. Staying on top of it might be boring, but *you're* not! Stand out!

Don't Just Be:

Be You in 3D

Are you as flat (and boring) as a page of text-based content?

Thanks to Internet blended search, you have an opportunity to present a 3D brand to the people you can't connect with face-to-face. Blended search means that images, video, and real-time content are displayed along with the standard written content we're used to—like links to blogs, websites, and articles.

Blended search has become increasingly common on major search engines, and it's one of the most exciting opportunities for career-minded executives since Tom Peters coined the term "personal branding" back in 1997. Blended search means you can give people who are googling you a much more accurate impression of who you are and what you have to offer.

According to Forrester Research, optimizing video and other rich media content to take advantage of blended search is by far the easiest way to get a first-page organic ranking on Google. And the "iProspect Blended Search Results Study," conducted by Jupiter Research, found that people searching the web are interested in multimedia and are "much more likely" to click on image, news, or video search results when they are presented in a blended format.

In this new world, it's wise to keep your web content diverse—from Twitter posts to multimedia. It's no longer enough to comment on a few blog posts, build your LinkedIn profile, and publish an article to a relevant website. Video helps you showcase your brand and build emotional connections with viewers. Images paint a picture of who you are and what you do.

William found that the multimedia website Reach launched, www.PersonalBranding.TV, has become the most popular of all Reach's web properties. The videos and audio files hosted there provide a much more valuable resource of "all things personal branding" than the Reach corporate website and blog combined!

Real-time, relevant, 3D content demonstrates that you are on top of what is happening in your industry or discipline, helps you showcase who you really are, and enables you to stand out in a Google search.

Are you expressing your brand with just the 26 letters of the alphabet, or with images, sounds, and actions?

DITCH | Wean yourself from the text habit; text-only information is old-school. Start creating and uploading images, videos, and multimedia content. If you're the first in your company to do so, that's OK. Lead the charge!

My Sparks

Record your ideas, sparked from Chapter 16.

Chapter Seventeen

Leverage LinkedIn, Facebook, and Twitte

GROW

Learn to Love LinkedIn

Befriend Facebook

Trust Twitter

Be Visible. Connect. Research:

Learn to Love LinkedIn

LinkedIn is a powerful business tool. Do you use it?

At over 200 million members and growing, and with members' professionally oriented searches expected to exceed 5.3 billion at the time of this book's publication, LinkedIn is Google for professionals. It's often the *first* place other professionals go to learn about you, *and* it's the first place you can go to do key parts of your job.

Need to find a qualified vendor? Leading a team and need a new member? Need to find potential clients or learn more about existing clients? Want to know more about your peers, and your manager, too? Looking to get promoted? Want to identify your competitors? Look to LinkedIn!

LinkedIn helps you do your job and makes your life as a career-minded executive easier because LinkedIn helps you to be visible, expand your connections, and perform research more easily. But do take care when sleuthing; if you want to be anonymous when using LinkedIn for researching others, change your privacy controls (you'll find them in Settings) so you don't leave your fingerprints behind!

And know that others are looking to LinkedIn, too—and they may be looking for you! When's the last time you visited your LinkedIn profile? If the last time you did was to change your job title to reflect your latest promotion, you've lost opportunities you didn't even know were there. Protect and perfect your profile—a great profile enables visibility and planned serendipity—because when you don't know who is looking for you, you need to be easy to find, with a 3D authenticity that entices connection.

To build a 3D view of YOU, try our top-10 LinkedIn tips:

1. Be a face! Post a professionally taken headshot, facing right—into your profile—not off to the left of the page.
2. Write your profile in third-person. Third-person (William's preference) makes it easier to brag and easier to be found in Google.
3. Or write your profile in first-person. First-person (Deb's preference) makes it easier to build chemistry and magnetic connection.
4. Brand it! Whether you are writing in first- or third-person, be you and infuse some personal into the professional.
5. Make your reader care! Focus on your impact, not your job description. Nothing bores a reader more than "responsible for..."
6. Verify your value. Ask for (and give) endorsements and recommendations.
7. Leverage your links. Connect the three hyperlinks located in Contact Info to your company website, YouTube channel, blog, articles, etc.
8. Be real! Embed one or more videos in your profile.
9. Highlight your skills. Choose those for which you want to be known and list them in the Skills and Expertise section.
10. Help people see who you are with Groups. Join relevant groups and participate for connection, visibility, and credibility.

Bonus tip: If you "need a kick in the career" (as Kirsten Dixson, William's co-author for *Career Distinction*, says), join the *Ditch. Dare. Do!* LinkedIn group for inspiration and connection to other career-minded professionals.

Are you visiting LinkedIn regularly?

DO | Pump up your profile! Do it now! LinkedIn is #1 for professional networking. Learn to love LinkedIn.

Be a Cautiously Open Book:
Befriend Facebook

Facebook is great for business and outstanding for your brand.

The line between work and life is blurring; so too is the line between social and professional networking. There was a time not too long ago when we advised our clients to use LinkedIn to network with professional contacts and Facebook to keep in touch with friends and family. Today, we recommend using LinkedIn for colleagues, and Facebook for everyone! Why? Because with almost a billion users, and a growing number of career-friendly features, Facebook has become a significant brand-building networking tool.

Whether you're a member of the "let it all hang out" clan—for whom the line between work and life has already disappeared—or a staunch believer in "keep my personal stuff personal!," Facebook can help your brand.

If you're comfortable with your professional contacts peering into your personal life, and vice versa, invite them to be Facebook friends. Craft a profile that is appropriate for business *and* social contacts—and be sure your posts reflect a relevant holistic mix of the social and professional you.

If you're in the "separate business and pleasure" camp, don't discount Facebook as a professional networking resource. In the early days of Facebook, you didn't have as much control over who saw what. Today, with its new features, Facebook can be a tool for managing your career and for sharing what happened over the weekend with your close friends. You can create custom groups, organize your friends into categories, and choose what you share with whom.

Facebook is a brand builder, but it can also be a brand buster. So whether you separate your professional contacts or merge them with your social contacts, plan and control your brand message.

Be brand-aware when you post photos—and remember that you can be tagged in others' photos, so be vigilant. Unless "ridiculous" is one of your brand attributes, you don't want your colleagues to see the goofy photo your wife shared with your family, or to find you tagged in an old college frat party shot that one of your friends just posted.

Here's another way you could lose control of your brand: It's tempting to click an interesting link when you see one included in a post or ad. But beware. When you click through, you usually can't connect to the site until you grant permission for that site to post on your behalf. Outsmart 'em: just copy the link and open a new window. Protect your strong brand.

And remember, no matter how busy you are, remain visible and valuable to your Facebook network. Regularly update your Facebook profile, begin and participate in conversations, "like" and comment, and contribute your own content. Strong brands don't go into hiding!

Are you ready to trade "Facebook is for friends and family" for "Facebook is good for my brand"?

DARE | Get outside your comfort zone and start using Facebook as a brand-building tool. Make a plan for increasing your visibility through the largest social network in the world.

Tweet Your Way to the Top: Trust Twitter

Forget what you've heard. Twitter's tweets are *not* for twits.

Some executives think Twitter is the place where you stalk celebrities or post what you had for breakfast. Others tell us saying something valuable in 140 characters is impossible. Still others think they have nothing to say on Twitter or avoid it as a time-sucking vortex of inanity. What's your take?

We say: Twitter is a valuable tool for business and a powerful resource for building your brand. Twitter means connection—of people and ideas. Deb and her co-authors of *The Twitter Job Search Guide*, Susan Whitcomb and Chandlee Bryan, call Twitter "the barrier buster" for its ability to leap-frog gatekeepers and get you connected with the people you need to know to help you build your brand. Chris Brogan, social media guru, speaks of Twitter as "the informational pulse." Tweets that demonstrate your expertise join that pulse, growing your network, influencing the people who want to know what you know, and initiating valuable relationships that can be expanded offline.

According to *Ad Age*, Tony Hsieh of Zappos fame has been an influential figure in demonstrating how Twitter can be used by C-level executives to build a connection with customers, partners, and employees. Think of *your* tweets as a giant brand-building billboard, pointing your followers to your thought leadership on the web (your blog posts, new YouTube videos, slide decks at SlideShare, or articles you've written), your offline professional activities, or interesting tweets others post.

Want to be visible to the media? Twitter is fast becoming the place writers go to find sources for stories; tweets get noticed by journalists, and yours can too. Want to know and/or comment on the latest trends? Do what journalists do: Perform a keyword search in Twitter and look for the latest tweets. Want to stay connected to customers in real time? Twitter helps you do it.

What should you tweet? It's simple: Tweet content that is valuable to your target audience and reinforces what you want to be known for. Focus on delivering great content, not on gathering followers. And generously retweet the valuable tweets of others. To paraphrase James Earl Jones's advice in the movie *Field of Dreams*, "Build it and they will come."

People connect with ideas, but they more often connect with people, so experts suggest an 80-20 ratio of professional to personal tweets. Personal tweets about hobbies, interests, and passions—even about who won *American Idol*, if that's a show you love—make you human. But be careful not to over-share. As our colleague and social media expert Chandlee Bryan advises, use "discretionary authenticity."

Be efficient; don't fritter with Twitter. Determine your strategy and content, and then use Twitter tools like HootSuite, TweetDeck and Twaitter to schedule tweets for a whole week or month, augmenting them with real-time tweets tied to today's topics. To make your tweets more searchable, attach a hashtag (the # symbol) to keywords or phrases, and use a URL shortener like bit.ly, goo.gl, or ow.ly to keep more of your 140 characters available for your wit and wisdom.

What's your first (or next) tweet going to say?

DITCH

Drop the "Twitter is for kids, nerds, and the birds" mindset. Repeat after us, with conviction: "Twitter is a business tool! Twitter is a business tool! Twitter is a business tool!"

My Sparks

Record your ideas, sparked from Chapter 17.

Chapter Eighteen

Build Your Brand on the Web

GROW

Blog to Bolster Your Brand

Build a Community on the Web

Get Others to Speak for You

Build Your Brand in Bits and Bytes:

Blog to Bolster Your Brand

Success requires you to be visible virtually. Period.

A well-written blog is a direct path to virtual visibility and better Google results. A blog lets you promote your ideas and accomplishments to communicate your value. It helps you build community with people who are critical to your doing your job. It will make you a more branded, attractive, quoted, and admired professional—and deepen your differentiation from other professionals who seemingly do what you do.

Some people don't blog because they worry that they don't know what to write, don't have enough content, don't have the writing skills, or don't want to write every day. We've heard it all—get over it! As an active professional, you always come across events, information, and activities that reinforce your beliefs; use these as content ideas and opportunities to express your unique and valuable message. You don't need to write every day; just be consistent and authentic (you can hire a ghostwriter if you need to).

Many people have ideas but are concerned that writing a blog will take too much time. Philippe, an IT systems manager, was excited about the thought of blogging but paralyzed by the fear that even a simple blog might become a full-time job—and he already had one of those. He pondered the problem and decided that there was a solution: He would make his blog a robust collaborative effort. He'd invite team members to become bloggers and feature diverse opinions about a single topic—customer service in IT. After a slow start, every member became a contributor. The blog took off and, as planned, the team expanded its external community of like-minded people. In addition, the team built stronger relationships with colleagues and with each other. The blog attracted media attention, which led to Philippe becoming a source for quotes in *CIO* and other IT magazines. Philippe's solution to his "blogging dilemma" increased brand-building visibility for himself, his team, and his company.

For Philippe, the subject of his blog—customer service in IT—was the easy part, but to fill daily posts, his team regularly brainstormed topic ideas that fit. If you need to find content ideas, set up Google alerts for topics that interest you. Follow trending topics on Twitter. Follow industry experts and thought leader blogs.

Another way to start blogging is to comment on the blog posts of these influencers—posts that interest you and are relevant to your stakeholders. It's often far easier to spontaneously write a cogent, passionate comment than to sit down to consciously write a blog post. Save your best comments and edit them into a blog post for your blog.

Continually adding to your blog keeps you cognizant of your industry, the marketplace, and the internal and external value of your ongoing contributions. You become more confident in your current position and better prepared for your next.

What do you care about, that your brand community cares about, that you can blog about?

DO

Build your blog. It's your own independent media outlet. Start with something you're passionate about that has value to your brand community. Jump in. Just do it!

Extend Your Brand Virtually:

Build a Community on the Web

In a world where even the smallest businesses can be global businesses, you need to be virtually visible.

Today, you are likely not co-located with your team members, yet your success requires that you be connected to the right resources at all times. That means that investing in virtual relationships is an essential part of doing your job.

And it's not hard. Social networks like LinkedIn, Twitter, Facebook, Google+, BranchOut—and any other social networks relevant to your industry or area of expertise—can help you expand your network and connect with members of your brand community. Strong brands use these networks and are sure to have a branded LinkedIn profile with recommendations and an array of groups, a BranchOut account with endorsements, a Twitter account with a branded background and 160-character profile, and a Google+ network.

When it comes to connecting, our advice is to trust your gut. If you're a very selective networker, you'll know who is on brand as a potential connection and who isn't. If you're a hungry power networker, go for it! You can let anyone you want into your network, but know that when you refer that person to another connection, you're putting your reputation on the line. When it comes to us, William is a power networker, but selectively refers. Deb is selective with both. And we're both right.

Joining groups on the web can be one of the best ways to expand your network. When William wrote his "Nine Minutes a Day: Continuous

Career Management" manifesto, LinkedIn sponsored it, published it, and established a companion "Nine Minutes" LinkedIn group. William joined the group and has connected with many coaches and careerists who share his continuous career management philosophy. Thanks to this focused virtual group, people from around the world—whom he would not have had the opportunity to know—are now part of William's network.

The social networking landscape changes as quickly as the weather in London. Some of the networks mentioned above didn't exist when we started writing this book, and others may likely be emerging as leaders by the time you read it. So stay abreast of emerging tools and technologies!

Are you virtually connected or virtually invisible?

DARE

S-t-r-e-t-c-h your social networking style. If you're a power networker, forge deeper connections. If you're a selective or reluctant networker, expand your circle.

Don't Pound Your Chest:

Get Others to Speak for You

Don't toot; let others tout!

Tooting your own horn. Pounding your chest. Singing your own praises. Bragging. Patting yourself on the back. These are not the ways to convince people of how accomplished you are.

The best way to build credibility and bolster your brand is to demonstrate what makes you exceptional. Then, nurture connections, build community, and have others speak for you.

The "Like" feature has been a part of sites such as Facebook, YouTube, and blogging software for a long time. When people "like" your content, they are endorsing you and making your ideas visible to a larger audience. LinkedIn has provided the opportunity to get and post recommendations from network members for years. And they recently added a feature that allows your network contacts to endorse your skills.

Some users of the online 360Reach™ personal branding survey bring their 360Reach report to performance reviews and interviews to show managers the feedback they received. (We first told you about 360Reach in Chapter 5, Snap 1.)

One of the 360Reach analysts recounts the story of a 360Reach user who received feedback that said his most successful team role was "leader." He was concerned that his manager saw him as more of a doer. Armed with this candid external feedback, he met with his boss and told her of his desire to take on management responsibility. He showed her the 360Reach comments that validated his leadership skills, and he put some of the comments from his 360Reach report on his blog, to make sure others knew of his leadership ability, too.

An increasing number of services focus primarily on reviewing professionals. Angie's List provides customer reviews, and lawyers.com provides peer review information; talent.me and connect.me allow you to anonymously evaluate your network members. Think about these services as "Trip Advisor for professionals." Soon, people will make decisions about you based on the collective opinions of others.

Recommendations, references, and testimonials have always been a necessary part of career management. Now, with this new class of tools, they will become even more important and more pervasive.

Do you come recommended?

DO | Collect testimonials; don't be shy or falsely modest. At the end of every project, and every time it makes sense, collect and convey feedback.

My Sparks

Record your ideas, sparked from Chapter 18.

Chapter Nineteen

GROW

Be Opportunistically Lazy

Be Real *and* Be Virtual

Make the Real, Virtual

Make the Virtual, Real

Maximize Your Message:

Be Real *and* Be Virtual

When you embrace your communications' real-virtual connection, your communications platform doubles down.

You get to be opportunistically lazy: with very little work, you can link and/or repurpose content from one world into the other, even from a previous "offline" existence. And in the words of Martha Stewart, "That's a good thing!"

Refreshing and repurposing "old" content, on- and offline, builds the consistency great brands share. And getting maximum mileage from past content instead of spending all your time developing new content leaves more time for other brand-building ditches, dares, and do's! That's a *really* good thing for a busy executive!

Here are just a few ways you can cross-pollinate your real and virtual brand communications:

Blogs

1. Include links to your blog posts in your articles.
2. Connect your blog posts with your YouTube videos and reference them in your real-world presentations.
3. Combine a few blog posts to create an article you can publish in print.

Presentations and Articles

1. Share your presentations online—on your website, LinkedIn, and Facebook.

2. Slice an article into a series of thought leadership tweets; then post them on Twitter.

3. Take online articles and incorporate the content into a presentation you deliver to local business groups or professional organizations.

LinkedIn and Your Website

1. Answer questions on LinkedIn; later, merge your LinkedIn answers into a how-to article.

2. Gather your performance evaluation feedback and transform it into testimonials for your website.

3. Get QR codes for real-world communications and link them to your home on the web.

Stay aligned and in focus as you create and mesh your real and virtual communication. Whether you're writing an article, preparing a presentation, writing a blog post, tweeting, or even commenting on a blog, it's important to know your brand and know your reader.

Don't muddy your brand track and skid off course with content that is unrelated to your brand and mission. Nothing kills a brand faster than irrelevancy.

Do you have a comprehensive and connected communications plan?

DITCH | Stop thinking that your real and virtual communications are different and separate. The lines between them are gone, replaced with a tide of brand-building, fluid connectivity. Jump in!

Increase Your Influence:

Make the Real, Virtual

Smart brands know that every *single* brand-building opportunity can be at least *10* opportunities in the virtual world!

Today, social media can propel traditional real-world communications to a new, expansive presence on the web. When you plan your next presentation, article, or other real-world communication, concurrently create a social media strategy to pump up its visibility and influence.

Here are *four* areas in which you can transform that *one* live activity into a virtual online campaign that can reach a thousand or even hundreds of thousands of people:

- **PR**—Write a press release about the activity and publish it on free press release search engines like prlog.org.
- **Social Media**—Update your Twitter, Facebook, and LinkedIn status with your presentation information. While presenting, encourage audience members to tweet, real-time. Send a "thank you" tweet to those who contributed to the conversation and to your presentation.
- **Crowdsourcing**—Via your blog or LinkedIn, ask your brand community to tell you what they'd like to learn in your presentation. While presenting, poll the audience to capture data related to your thought leadership. Use the data you culled from your audience for blog posts; share these via Twitter.
- **Video and Slide Sharing**—Arrange to have your presentation filmed. After the conference, post the video clips to your

YouTube channel (and to sites like Vimeo and Blip.tv). Post your presentation slides to sites like sliderocket.com and then tweet the links.

Lee, a shy but confident events manager in the Midwest, made "the real, virtual" when she took a "double-dare" leap outside her comfort zone. She decided to "dare" to deliver a presentation to her local American Marketing Association chapter, entitled, "Using Social Media to Increase Event Attendance." Then, taking on another "dare," she invited a videographer to film her and produce a video of her 45-minute talk.

Lee was so happily surprised by her professional and assertive video presence that she took her top five clips and posted them online. They routinely show up on page one when someone googles her. Now, that's being opportunistically lazy!

Are you using the multiplier effect to increase your influence?

DITCH | Get over any bias against social media; then use social media to expand your offline presence into powerful online professional visibility opportunities.

Build a Book (and More):
Make the Virtual, Real

Nothing builds brand credibility better than a book; white papers, reports, articles, presentations, and videos do, too!

As a busy executive already stretched thin, how do you find the time to write at length? You don't need to quit your job to make it happen. If you've been posting thought leadership on the web, your work is about to pay off—because collecting, collating, coordinating, combining, and curating content from past posts is an invaluable way to become an opportunistically lazy (and prolific) writer!

Poaching and editing your existing online thought leadership makes it easy to take your voice from the *virtual* world to the *real* world. Chances are your online ideas, thoughts, and messages are still valid. Refresh them and weave them into something else—from new online postings to offline white papers, reports, or even that dream book.

In fact, you're probably closer to that book than you think. If you've been tweeting twice a day for two years, you have written the equivalent of a quarter of a book. If blogging is your preferred tool for communicating, there are countless books, videos, and blogs devoted to creating a book from your blog posts—or you might use these seven steps to blog to build a book (and your brand):

1. Choose a subject that is on-brand, has a market, and is interesting to you. Being "jump-out-of-your-skin" excited about your subject will keep you motivated!

2. Choose a list of topics that fit neatly under your subject, create a draft TOC, and turn them into blog categories.

3. To create the topics you will research and write about, identify 6 to 10 relevant sub-topics for each category—and remember to establish Google alerts on these keywords; you'll stay on top of related content.

4. Establish a writing schedule and stick to it. No one is waiting for your book to come out, so you need to create your own blog-posting deadlines—and meet them!

5. Build your blog community. Use their feedback and comments to refine your topics and material.

6. To begin your manuscript, pull from your blog content. Then add fresh content, create transitions, refine the material, and make it read like a bestseller!

7. Work with an agent or self-publishing company to go from manuscript to book (or eBook)!

Then go beyond books. Take what you do online and think about how you can turn it into a real-world brand-builder. One of William's clients turns his tweets into top-10 lists that he includes in his team presentations. We know a management consultant who took all the book reviews that she posted at Amazon.com and created a report on her area of thought leadership, and we learned of an executive who transformed his YouTube videos into a show reel DVD to promote his expertise to the media.

Are you ready to poach your posts?

DARE

Trust that you CAN write your masterpiece without quitting your job! Find everything you have posted on the web; gather it into a document or slides, and then turn all that hard work into your dream book or other real-world communications.

My Sparks

Record your ideas, sparked from Chapter 19.

Chapter Twenty

Use Video to Be There

GROW

- Use Video to Express Yourself
- Make Video Calls
- Use Video to Break Through

Get Ready for Your Close-up:

Use Video to Express Yourself

A video bio is the next best thing to a personal introduction.

According to renowned professor and psychologist Dr. Albert Mehrabian, words account for only 7% of a communication. So written bios are quite limited by having only words to tell the world who you are. Video allows you to add body language and inflection to those words, to deliver a complete, memorable communication. It's the ideal tool for introducing yourself to people you can't meet in person, with a message that's more clear, compelling, and personal than the written word.

A video version of your bio allows you to project your personal brand in 3D—to communicate those visual and emotional personal brand attributes that will get people interested in you, and to say all of the important things that people are usually left to read between the lines. And with the ubiquity of video-sharing sites like YouTube, Vimeo, and TubeMogul, it's easy to widely share your video bio and to grow your network by allowing online contacts to view your video.

"If you look at the evolution and visualization of the online profile, the world is changing so rapidly that it is hard to keep up," says Catharine Fennell, founder/CEO of videoBIO. "It used to be that adding a headshot to LinkedIn or Facebook was a nice thing to have. Now, without a headshot on your online profiles, people start to question 'Why no picture?' Video is the new standard in the way to represent your brand *and your ideas* online. It conveys your message in a way that a picture cannot do. And, like your brand, video content is not static—it's constantly evolving."

One of the biggest misconceptions about video is that it has to follow a conventional format. That's just not the case. Video should be used to amplify your message—whatever it is you want to communicate. And remember, it's about content first; it's not about being perfect. Making a connection and delivering an authentic message is what will capture the attention of your audience. Produce a video bio to convey who you are, what you're passionate about, and what you want people to know about you. Express your voice and personal style, plus intangibles like humor, wit, enthusiasm, empathy, and energy.

As the world becomes more virtual, and many professionals get comfortable with using video as a way of connecting and expressing ideas, video bios will be a standard career-marketing tool. Yet, to many people, "video" equals "vulnerable." In fact, we think that as video becomes a standard communication tool, fear of appearing in a video will be as prevalent (and paralyzing) as fear of public speaking. The same strategies we suggested in Chapter 15 (Snap 2) to help overcome fear of public speaking apply here: Practice, practice, practice; join an organization like Toastmasters; and consider engaging a coach.

Video killed the radio star, as the British new-wave group The Buggles sang, but we promise it won't kill your career. It will breathe new life into it!

Will you be among the first wave of executives to use a video bio, or will you struggle to catch up?

DARE | Overcome your reticence; accept video as your friend. Use content from your brand bio for your video bio script. Then smile and get in front of the camera.

Email Is *SO* Last Century:
Make Video Calls

Email is just not appropriate for real-time communication.

Since words account for the smallest percentage of a communication, email—and its ugly cousin, instant messaging—are not always the best communication tools. Both are inefficient, boring, and, ironically, disconnecting. Of course, a telephone call can be more effective for real-time communications than email or instant messaging, but it still won't deliver a complete communication experience.

If you're a friend to people in far-flung places, or part of a family living in other states or countries, you've already had that complete communication experience via Skype, FaceTime, Google+, or another visual interaction tool. Yet if you are working in a major corporation, email, instant messaging, and phone calls are probably what you and your colleagues use most, even when you know that video calls enable more satisfying and productive communication.

With the challenges of today's virtual workplace, doesn't it make sense to take what you already do at home to work? To make video calls your default? And today, every workplace is virtual; whether you're teaming with colleagues around the globe or instant messaging a colleague in the next office or cubicle, the effect is the same: "Same space" interaction is on the decline.

When you are not co-located with many of the people you work with daily—or often use phone, email, or instant messaging to save the time it takes to walk down the hall for a conversation—you can see the importance of using a communications vehicle that is truly human, truly connective, *and* truly efficient. And of course, real-time video calls and meetings are excellent ways to be there without having to head out to the airport.

And William is in a lot of airports! His travel schedule and Deb's location made collaboration on this book a challenge. The manuscript for this book was written during infrequent day-long in-person meetings in various coffee shops and hotel lobbies in New York City, and those meetings were augmented by video calls. This was a valuable way to maintain momentum, stay focused, and stay connected. And Deb was happy that during video calls, William (who freely admits to having the attention span of a toddler) could not easily engage in the multitasking he so often does when on the phone.

With Cisco Telepresence, Skype, FaceTime, Google+, and other emerging tools, we predict it won't be long before video dominates the communications landscape at most companies, as it is already doing at tech-savvy start-ups and innovative organizations.

For now, most people will default to their usual communication tools. And that's good for you. When others are on the fence about video calling, you'll be the early adopter—video will be *your* real-time communications tool to truly stand out.

Are you willing to invest just a little more time and effort to powerfully express your brand through real-time video?

DO | Integrate video into your daily communications. Lead your team into the future. Now. Do it before you look like a dinosaur!

The Medium Is the Message:

Use Video to Break Through

Video not only gets *you* noticed, it gets your *ideas* noticed.

Do you have a proposal to submit to an internal or external client? An important communication you want to send to your team? A product or process you need to describe? A lesson you need to teach? A message you want your boss to pay attention to? Using video or a combination of communication vehicles—text, images, and video—is a great way to stand out while delivering a more powerful, human, and effective message.

With the ubiquity of video creation, sharing, and distribution tools, producing a video or multimedia communication is nearly as easy as producing a report, and it delivers a much greater impact. Just turning a PowerPoint presentation into a narrated video can help your idea stand out and get noticed. And it helps you build your brand attribute of current, creative, visionary, or tech-savvy.

One of William's clients, Suzanne, a feisty woman with a real people focus, wanted to demonstrate the benefits of reorganizing the marketing team—creating an integrated team of marketing generalists instead of a group of independently focused specialists. It was a truly contentious topic, and previous discussions about the change were—to say the least—unproductive. So Suzanne decided to create a video using infographics, interviews with marketing staff, quotes from organization development experts, and a compelling theme—"Integrate, Don't Insulate." She put it on a USB key and mailed it to her manager with a heartfelt note about how strongly she felt about its contents. Her manager was impressed and agreed to a beta-test of her proposal. She's confident her recommendations will be fully accepted!

Get comfortable with using video to pitch *your* ideas—to inspire, engage, and inform—and get your video tools in order. You'll need a video camera (or your phone or computer), basic editing tools, and hosting and sharing website accounts—like YouTube, Vimeo, videoBIO, and TubeMogul (if you don't have an internal repository at your company). These tools, once reserved for movie producers, are now becoming a standard part of the branded executive's toolkit!

Have you ever perused SlideShare? If you haven't, take a few moments to check it out. Type the keywords related to your area of expertise—what you want to be known for—into the search box and watch a few of the presentations that come up. Impressed? Think you can do better? *We* think you can. So why are you leaving it to others to tell the world about *your* topic? Isn't it time you shared your point of view in a compelling way?

Before sending any important communication, ask yourself if video is the better way to get your idea across.

Could video be your new killer app?

DITCH | Forget internal or express mail. The next time you have something really important to say, use video to send *a* message with *the* message.

My Sparks

Record your ideas, sparked from Chapter 20.

Chapter Twenty-One GROW

Widen Your Web

Build Relationships

Give to Get

Get Involved

Life Is Who You Know:

Build Relationships

The value of your social capital is directly proportional to the depth and breadth of your relationships.

More and more, you need to be connected to a network of resources for mutual benefit and growth—for yourself and for your organization. But do you know who is already in your network? And how do you know whom or what you need in your network?

Whether internal or external, relationships don't just happen. Revisit your goals. Do a network "gap analysis." Think about critical decision-makers and influencers—the people, positions, and companies you need in your network to help you do your job and reach your goals—and then craft strategies to get on their radar. Seek out opportunities in the real and virtual world to reconnect with, or encounter, "your" people. Participate in professional associations; contribute to thought leaders' blogs; join alumni, industry, and job function groups; get active in LinkedIn and Twitter; and build a professional presence on Facebook.

Look for networking opportunities that others just don't see. During his workshops, William often asks participants to share their most creative idea for adding people to their network. At one workshop in Dallas, Gustavo screamed out, "Give blood." Intrigued, William asked him to share more. Gustavo went on to say that every time his company has a blood drive, he is among the first to volunteer to donate. When giving blood, he's there for 20 to 30 minutes with nothing to do but hang out with people from throughout the company that he otherwise wouldn't meet! Although Gustavo is in product development, he's branded as the guy who knows everyone in the company—and his secret is that he met most of them while doing something that makes him feel good. Gustavo says, "My motto is give blood, get connected."

Like Gustavo, don't think of networking as something you do in addition to everything on your daily do-list; think about how you incorporate networking into everything you do! And when you do make connections, cement them. William takes photos at the association events he attends, and then uses the iPhone app Touchnote to turn those photos into relationship-building opportunities. Touchnote allows you to send a photo to a service that creates a custom, hardcopy postcard and mails it with your personal message. William chooses the perfect photos, collects the business cards of the people he meets, and sends them postcard reminders of the event they attended.

Networking doesn't take *away* time from your job—networking is *part* of your job. Your value in the *outside* world makes you more powerful and successful *inside* the walls of your company. When people know who you are and what you are about, opportunities come your way. It's planned serendipity!

Have you done a gap analysis? Do you know who needs to know you? Or with whom you need to reconnect?

DARE | Leave the office early to attend a function where "your people" will be present. Build three new relationships while you are there, and commit to keeping them going. You never know where they'll have *you* going!

Networking Is Not All about You:

Give to Get

The approach to building and maintaining a valuable network involves giving, not taking.

Give to get. Serve to sell. What goes around comes around. Successful networking is all about career karma—your social capital. The best networkers understand the value of investing—of nurturing their networks to grow their social capital.

They do a little bit of investing—of "giving"—each day, making new contacts while adding value to their existing network. When you approach networking from the perspective of giving, you build long-lasting relationships. Think of it as making deposits in your investment account and emergency fund. The more you add to your account, the more you give to your network, the more powerful and valuable it becomes. And unlike your 401(k), its value rarely decreases. With constant attention and care, your network will be there when you truly need it.

Investing in relationships is good business. Relationships help you source staff, solve problems that cannot be solved internally, benchmark your internal processes, provide perspective on emerging trends, and open doors that would otherwise be bolted shut. An internal network can help your career path in your organization, and your external network can give you visibility that helps your career and your company.

A few years ago, one of Deb's clients, whom we'll call Imran, returned to the United States after many years working abroad. He'd declined a promotion he didn't want, resigned on good terms, and stayed on for six months to train his successor. Imran had always been in demand and wasn't concerned about a job search—but after his resignation, the U.S. economy went from boom to gloom. By the time he stepped on U.S. soil, the country was in a swiftly deepening recession. He needed a network, and fast. Imran quickly reestablished contact with his U.S. connections, they shifted into high gear, and he landed a position in months, in the downturn, when executive job searches were trending upwards of a year.

How did Imran do it? His network was a reserve of capital, and his regular deposits were the connections he enabled—brokering introductions to people he knew who might benefit from knowing each other. He was memorable for his agenda-less generosity. When he needed help, his network rallied around him. People liked him, respected him, and wanted to help.

Weave a strong web and connect others within *your* network. Be a matchmaker. Mentally sort through your contacts when you meet someone new. Think about who they should meet and the mutual value you can create by connecting them.

How have you given to YOUR network today?

DO

Purposefully and significantly grow your network's value. Implement one network-nurturing activity each day, for seven days. Continue for a month to build a network-nurturing habit. Some habits are good. This is one of them.

Don't Sit on the Sidelines:
Get Involved

Strong brands contribute to the world at large.

Corporate social responsibility is a strong thread in the fabric of the modern corporation. American Express is committed to ending hunger, Avon supports breast cancer awareness, and Benetton supports global understanding. And Blake Mycoskie doesn't even see a difference between what his company, TOMS Shoes, does and how it helps society. According to the *Chronicle of Philanthropy*, the thirtysomething entrepreneur says he's not running a company; he's spearheading a global movement by harnessing the power of consumers to do good.

Just as branding is no longer limited to products and organizations, owning a cause isn't limited to the business world. Personal social responsibility is not only a big part of giving back, it's a big part of branding.

Olympic gold medalist Shaun White is as focused on charitable work as he is on skateboarding. He supports the Tony Hawk Foundation, Make-A-Wish Foundation, and Summit on the Summit. The Ryan Seacrest Foundation is devoted to using the power of interactive multimedia to enhance the quality of life for seriously ill and injured children; Christina Aguilera supports human rights through her work as a UN ambassador for the World Food Programme; former President Jimmy Carter builds houses for Habitat for Humanity. And you probably know other people who are wholeheartedly connected to a cause.

Luanne Tierney, the Juniper Networks executive you met in Chapter 8, is committed to helping underprivileged kids get an education, get to college, and get to work—and she brought that cause to *her* work. She convinced her company to hold ice cream socials to raise money for Students Rising Above (SRA), and she recently hosted a Women in Tech Leadership program, bringing some of the kids from SRA to attend and learn. Luanne has raised $75,000 for SRA since becoming involved with their program, and organizing the socials connects her to people from outside her organization who get to know her and her company in a fun way. William asked her if the ice cream interferes with her brand attribute of "physically fit," and she told him, "Ice cream is one of my favorite treats! Being physically fit doesn't mean you can't selectively indulge."

Doing good is usually a part of doing well. Being involved with others is good for you, good for society, and good for your brand. When you contribute to a cause about which you are passionate, you increase your energy, drive, and perspective. You become attractive to those around you. You learn skills you can bring to work. You make connections that enhance your network and add meaning to life.

Strong brands give of themselves. They are a part of the fabric of society.

What's your cause?

DARE | Give yourself permission to step away from work to do something that is not directly related to the daily grind. Moving a cause forward moves you forward. And it's fulfilling and fun! You remember fun, right?

My Sparks

Record your ideas, sparked from Chapter 21.

My GROW

Go-time Grid

Learning has little value without action!

Go back to the ditch, dare, and do sparks that you documented after each chapter in GROW. Break them into tasks you can put on your "do-list." Use the table below to describe the task, assign it a priority, and note the date by which you will complete it.

You can document your thoughts here, or download the PDF version of this chart at ditchdaredo.com/resources.

Ditch, Dare, or Do	Priority	Concrete action I will take	What do I want to achieve from it?	Date

Ditch, Dare, or Do	Priority	Concrete action I will take	What do I want to achieve from it?	Date

Ditch. Dare. Do!

DONE?

Not quite!

It's GO Time!

Personal branding is fun, rewarding, and fulfilling. It's also not for the fainthearted or unprepared.

Like a great athlete, you need to understand the environment you're working in and then prepare yourself—physically and mentally—before you immerse yourself in the branding process.

Athletes invest in the best coaches. Executives and companies do, too. You're no different; you'll need to invest time and effort in the preparation required for brand "strength training."

When you do, you'll be ready to build your brand. Excel in a rapidly changing (even harsh) environment, deliver what your company needs, and—at the same time—achieve professional success, fulfillment, and, yes, even real happiness, in the face of omnipresent challenges.

And the challenges are many. What worked yesterday doesn't work today. The world of work has changed forever and continues to change at an ever-increasing rate.

As an executive, the marketplace is your brand's proving ground—a muddy scrimmage field, elite training facility, and mega-stadium.

Are you ready to compete?

QUICK QUIZ

Before you line up at the starting gate, rate your readiness.

Are you ready for GO time?				
Strongly Disagree				**Strongly Agree**
I am ready to commit at least nine minutes a day to building my personal brand and to supporting my organization's brand.				
1	2	3	4	5
I will reach out to and collaborate with experts who can help me reach my personal goals and those of my company.				
1	2	3	4	5
I am committed to growing and evolving my brand in response to my personal growth and the inevitable changes in the marketplace.				
1	2	3	4	5
I will plan my work and work my plan to make an immediate branded impact in any new position I take.				
1	2	3	4	5
I will participate in at least one development program each year that will keep my brand current, relevant, and compelling.				
1	2	3	4	5

Total: ______

If you didn't score a 25—and our highest-achieving, hardest-working, most career-focused clients typically don't—read on so you can create your go-plan!

What Are You Waiting For?

GO

Engage Experts

Do Something. Now!

EVOLVE!

Plan Your Work:
Engage Experts

The new status symbol is not the products you buy; it's the experts you engage.

Accountant. Attorney. Financial Advisor. Housekeeper. Gardener. Tax Advisor. Nanny. Executive Assistant. Personal Trainer. Dog Walker.

All the personal services you can imagine are available. There's someone to help you select your suit, tailor it so it fits perfectly, drop it at the dry cleaner when it's dirty, and pick it up when it's clean. And there is an assistant to manage virtually every other aspect of your life, too.

Your salary is paying for all of those *personal* services. But when it comes to how you earn, how you spend most of your waking life, and how you gain your satisfaction and fulfillment, do you ever consider investing some of that salary in expert professionals who can help you put your best foot forward, nurture your career, and get everything you deserve? Most people don't, to their detriment.

Career-minded executives happily invest in experts who will help them build, support, and evolve their personal brands. Here's just a brief list of the types of professionals they often engage:

- ☐ Executive brand coach
- ☐ Career consultant
- ☐ Internal and/or external mentor
- ☐ Internal coach
- ☐ PR/media coach
- ☐ Ghostwriter

☐ Image consultant

☐ Executive recruiter

☐ Agent

Karen Friedman, a Philadelphia-based communications expert and author of *Shut Up and Say Something,* tells the story of an executive who called her on behalf of one of his strongest employees. He was concerned that this key employee was in danger of losing his job because he lacked executive presence and was not in command of his material when addressing senior management.

"The caller's company was in the middle of a hostile takeover, and his valued employee was in jeopardy because he was not seen as a commanding communicator," Karen said. "So over the next several months, the employee and I worked face-to-face until he learned how to connect with and empower others. Not only is he now perceived as a confident communicator, but the head of the new, merged company promoted him to a major position for which he would never have been considered previously. He decided to continue to work with me to take his communications skills to the next level!"

Strong brands aren't loners, so why work alone? Use the knowledge and support of experts to help you build and execute your brand plan.

Which experts do you need to engage?

DITCH | Drop the go-it-alone mindset. Engage the people you need to move your brand forward.

Work Your Plan:
Do Something. Now!

Time frames are shrinking. For everything. Yet the stakes are higher every day.

You need to prove yourself in a shorter time. Whether you have been assigned to a new project, have a new team leader, or have been put on a new account, you have no time to waste getting up to speed. And you must deliver value in your current role while perpetually preparing for your next position.

Even at the highest levels of the organization, you have a shrinking window of opportunity in which to make an impression. According to Mindy Lubber, in an article on *Forbes.com* entitled "Ending Quarterly Capitalism," "Average CEO tenure has dropped from eight to four years over the past generation..." And research from executive search firm Spencer Stuart found that a CMO's average stay in America's top corporations ranged from just 22 to 42 months, depending upon the industry.

You must deliver results from the *second* you arrive. You can't rely on someone to tell you what to do or how to do it. The CEO's 100-day action plan is no longer just for CEOs. No matter what your job function or level, you must show up on day one of a new job, project, or activity with a branded plan for that day and for the following 99 days as well.

One of Deb's clients, "Jorge," was happily employed but wanted to relocate and was in pursuit of his dream job—a job with the leading company in his field, headquartered in his desired location. He researched the company thoroughly, networked into it through a connection, and already had a potential plan to discuss during the interview. His preparedness and unique ideas spurred an offer, and he was slated to start in six weeks.

In those six weeks, although not on the payroll, Jorge thoroughly questioned all his reports, his new boss, his vendors, and his predecessor. By the first day of his job, he had gone into action with a list of stretch goals and a plan to accomplish them within the year. He and the team were off and running. His results catalyzed innovation and profit—and earned him two major promotions in two years.

Like Jorge, we are all leaders and can no longer expect to be told what to do or how to do it. The "command and control" leadership model of the industrial age has no relevance in our experiential, multigeneration, dynamic workplace of today. We're expected to figure it out, and we have to deliver it NOW. Scary? Maybe. Exciting? Absolutely.

Having a plan is part of building a reputation that gives you the freedom to *work* your plan—to quickly embed your impact into the fabric of the organization. When you do this, you are a leader; you create branded buzz in the organization; you are seen as a good hire—and an investment that is paying off. You'll soon be thought of as a seasoned employee—even if it's so early that you still count your tenure in weeks.

Are you ready to publish your plan, make it visible to your boss, and act on it?

DARE | Don't wait for direction. Plan your work and work your plan. Fast. You'll fly past the command and control crowd.

Build Momentum: EVOLVE!

What works today may not work tomorrow.

Everything changes. We change. Our companies change. Our goals change. The world changes. The only constant IS change.

3D personal branding may be the single most important tool for managing change. And branding is achievable for everyone, especially executives. While corporate branding typically requires scores of ad execs and million-dollar marketing budgets, personal branding requires only you (although an executive brand coach can make the process far less daunting and far more fun and effective).

Yet branding isn't a one-time process. To remain relevant and compelling, you and your brand must evolve. Just as advertising and marketing change to better meet consumer needs and desires, your brand can't stay static. Your brand must retain vibrancy to continue to deliver value.

It's easy to become distracted by the many demands of work and life. But stay focused, and don't be surprised by a faltering brand; continually assess its viability. Vigilant self-reflection and awareness of your surroundings contribute to understanding, evolving, and protecting your brand.

Pat, an attorney at a major law firm, realized this one day when she said, "I looked up and saw that my job was no longer about managing employee utilization rates (UR); it was about relationships." Pat was known for having one of the highest URs in the firm, but she acknowledged that her role had evolved and her focus needed to be about building long-term relationships *outside* the firm. "I finally got my head around the fact that what made me successful in the past was not going to make me a partner in the firm. I needed to spend less time on UR spreadsheets and more time meeting with clients and prospects. I needed to get out of my office and expand my skills in relationship building."

No one can predict what will happen in the world, the economy, your company, or your department. And even the most self-aware among us cannot predict our changing interests, desires, or opportunities. Yet because the branding process is recursive, the more you question, remain open, and stay connected to what's happening around you, the better your chances of becoming or remaining successful as you and your brand evolve.

It's up to you and your brand to keep momentum in the morass of confusion that is work today. Pat realized this: To rebrand from a "UR quant" to an executive on the partner track, she took a relationship-building course, made a commitment to reconnect with clients from the past, and hosted informational meetings at the firm for all current clients.

Assess your brand relevance every quarter. Identify a new skill, opportunity, or action that is critical to remaining relevant. Then, like Pat, act on it.

Is your brand toughing it out today, or trending towards tomorrow?

DARE | If your brand is faltering, be courageous. Change! If *you* want to be seen as relevant and valuable, take the bold steps needed to keep your *brand* relevant and valuable.

My Sparks

Record your ideas, sparked from Chapter 22.

My GO

Go-time Grid

Learning has little value without action!

Go back to the ditch, dare, and do sparks that you documented after each chapter in GO. Break them into tasks you can put on your "do-list." Use the table below to describe the task, assign it a priority, and note the date by which you will complete it.

You can document your thoughts here, or download the PDF version of this chart at ditchdaredo.com/resources.

Ditch, Dare, or Do	Priority	Concrete action I will take	What do I want to achieve from it?	Date

Ditch, Dare, or Do	Priority	Concrete action I will take	What do I want to achieve from it?	Date

AFTERWORD

We wrote *Ditch. Dare. Do!* for YOU.

We wrote it because we KNOW branding lets you show the world your best self. We KNOW branding is the single best way to become happier and more successful. We KNOW branding yourself will make your company more successful, too.

How do we know? We've seen it all. And we've seen branding work... again, and again, and again.

We have seen executives ready to give up and retire become re-energized. We have seen professionals lacking confidence in what they are doing become rabid evangelists for their internal causes.

We have seen leaders lost in the tangle of the corporate jungle forge new paths, once they bring who they really are to work. We have seen people burned out, defeated, underappreciated, overworked, and just plain miserable find ways to easily capture joy.

Personal branding worked for all of them. It rescued, restored, reinvigorated, and reinforced them.

We've also seen people already so excited and jazzed by their jobs that they wanted more, and more, and more... and personal branding worked for them, too.

Personal branding will work for YOU.

Personal branding works if you do it.

So do it!

You know what to do...

You know you can do it...

You know when you can do it (in nine minutes a day!)...

You know what doing it will do for you...

What are you waiting for?

Go forth and brand! Be...

- ☐ authentic
- ☐ bold
- ☐ clear
- ☐ compelling
- ☐ competent
- ☐ consistent
- ☐ daring
- ☐ deliberate
- ☐ emotional
- ☐ fearless
- ☐ found
- ☐ generous
- ☐ genuine
- ☐ great
- ☐ happy
- ☐ indestructible
- ☐ indispensable
- ☐ influential
- ☐ irresistible
- ☐ joyful
- ☐ loved
- ☐ open
- ☐ opinionated
- ☐ passionate
- ☐ real
- ☐ relevant
- ☐ strong
- ☐ successful
- ☐ trusted
- ☐ unique
- ☐ valuable
- ☐ viable
- ☐ visible

☐ YOURSELF!

INDEX

ABOUT THE AUTHORS

William Arruda

A citizen of the world with boundless energy and a genuine passion for human potential, William Arruda is a personal branding pioneer, bestselling author, and public speaker. He is credited with turning the concept of personal branding into a global industry, and his leadership in the field has inspired thousands of coaches to become personal branding strategists. His company, Reach, is the global leader, with consultants in 31 countries and 20% of the Fortune 100 as clients.

William is one of the most sought-after speakers on career development, social media, and, of course, personal branding. He has delivered hundreds of lively, motivational keynotes and workshops to audiences of 5 to 5,000 throughout the Americas, Europe, Asia and Africa. He's still waiting for his invitation to Antarctica! His client list reads like the pages of *Fortune* magazine: Adobe, BMW, British Telecom, GE, IBM, JPMorgan, Microsoft, Morgan Stanley, Target, and Starwood Hotels are just a few in a long list of corporate clients. His private clients include some of the world's most influential leaders.

William has been featured on the BBC, the Discovery Channel, NPR, and Fox News, and in *Forbes*, *Time*, and *Entrepreneur*. He is the author of the bestselling book *Career Distinction* (J. Wiley). He has lived in Boston, London, and Paris and now calls New York City home. He holds a master's degree in education. William exudes optimism and a genuine belief in the power each of us has to achieve great things. He not only sees the glass as half full; he sees the potential for it to be overflowing.

Connect with William at williamarruda@reachcc.com, or learn more at www.williamarruda.com or on Twitter @williamarruda.

Deb Dib

Known as the CEO Coach, Deb Dib is an early and unapologetically passionate advocate of leveraging the power of personal branding for 3D executive success. Her sweet spot is intense career-momentum branding for disruptive innovators, no-box thinkers, and gutsy leaders with a conscience who "Do capitalism right." She positions these leaders and rising stars to "land faster, earn more, have fun, and change the world!" which strongly supports her clients' goals while also supporting *her* goal: "Changing the world, one executive at a time!"

A Master Brand Strategist, thought leader, speaker, and educator, Deb is the founder of C-suiteCareerCatalysts.com, a consortium of top career professionals focusing on C-level careers; co-creator (with Susan Whitcomb) of The Academies' *Get Clear. Get Found. Get Hired!* coach certification program; and co-author of the award-winning book, *The Twitter Job Search Guide*.

Deb's work is featured in 30 career books, and her advice has appeared in articles in *The Washington Post, The New York Times, The Wall Street Journal, The Daily News, Newsday, Forbes.com, Money.com*, and *BusinessWeek.com*, among others.

A recognized innovator and one of the first Reach Certified Personal Branding Strategists, Deb was honored to be the first recipient of the Dick Bolles/Career Management Alliance Parachute Award for "sustained, enduring, and innovative contribution."

Deb's love of language, passion for change, collaborative nature, tough yet caring coaching style, and sense of the ridiculous run deep. They are traits inherited from her "social-activist" librarian parents, and "management" skills learned as the eldest of nine rambunctious children!

Connect with Deb at debdib@executivepowerbrand.com, www.executivepowerbrand.com, www.C-suiteCareerCatalysts.com, or on Twitter @CEOcoach.

CPSIA information can be obtained at www.ICGtesting.com
Printed in the USA
LVOW050739150513

333836LV00001B/23/P

9 781620 504574